Richard
Peter
Hoffman

A Pennsylvania German Precisionist

THE ART OF
Richard Peter Hoffman

With Critical Essays by
Mahlon H. Hellerich and Scott T. Swank

Birdsboro, Pennsylvania
An occasional publication of The Pennsylvania German Society
1990

This volume was produced for distribution to the members of The Pennsylvania German Society and to friends of Richard Peter Hoffman.

Project Coordinator: *Mahlon H. Hellerich*
Editor: *Frederick S. Weiser*
Design & Production: *Musselman Advertising, Inc.*
Printer: *Kutztown Publishing Company, Kutztown*

Cover: **The Artist's Challenge, July 1951**
Hoffman's drawing ability is showcased in a painting of exceptional three-dimensional quality. This is a powerful personal image as well—perhaps a symbolic self-portrait — which offers a rare glimpse into the inner world of the artist at the moment of satisfaction when one artistic challenge has been met and a clean canvas awaits the next creation.

Richard at Work, ca. 1960

6

RICHARD PETER HOFFMAN

A Biographical Sketch

by Mahlon H. Hellerich

RICHARD PETER HOFFMAN WAS BORN ON JANUARY 10, 1911 TO GEORGE MOSES HOFFMAN AND STELLA WOTRING HOFFMAN IN THE FAMILY HOME at 1345 Turner Street in Allentown, Pennsylvania. Hoffman was an eighth-generation Pennsylvania German. In his immediate family background were four large, prominent and well-established families of Lehigh County—the Hoffman, Hollenbach, Wotring and Krause clans. His father, George Moses, was born and raised on the Rinker farm, near Neffs, on which his grandfather worked as a tenant farmer. Hoffman's mother, Stella Polly Wotring, was born and raised on a farm near Newside, a small village in the vicinity of Slatington. Apparently, their experiences as farm children taught both parents the importance of hard work, self-discipline, frugality and self-reliance in the attainment of a satisfying and secure life, preferably in an urban setting. George Moses' first job was as a clerk in a grocery store in Slatington. He soon moved to Allentown where he worked as a clerk at Koch Brothers, the leading men's clothing store in town. George and Stella were married in May 1910 and set up housekeeping at 1345 Turner Street. Richard D. Wotring, Stella's father, had established himself by that time as a successful realtor in Allentown and lived nearby with his family at 1357 Turner. He may have been helpful in facilitating the move of his daughter and son-in-law to Allentown and in starting in business.

In 1911, George Moses opened a grocery store at Tenth and Turner Streets in Allentown. He became a successful merchant and businessman. He invested his life in his store and in the cause of the independent grocer; he earned a satisfying return on his investment financially and in community recognition of his business acumen and enterprise. After giving birth to Richard Peter, Stella Polly opened a millinery shop on the west side of North Seventh Street between Linden and Turner Streets. She also was a successful manager and her shop was so well-patronized that she employed as many as ten hat trimmers. She remained in business until the mid-1920s when readymade hats became popular. Both parents were aggressive and creative shopkeepers, able to found, direct and lead prosperous, small businesses. Richard Peter was their only child.

Richard Peter Hoffman, age 6

His mother's involvement with her store meant that Richard Peter was raised by nannies. He remembers three women who cared for him at various times: Mrs. Redline, Mrs. Unangst and Mrs. Rosie Ritter, whom he recalls with great fondness. He was frequently taken to mother's store as a young boy where he spent many enjoyable hours. He also spent much time with his Wotring grandmother at 1357 Turner. At home, at grandmother's and at the store, the women fussed over him. Later, when he was in elementary school, he would come to his mother's shop after school and remain with her until closing time. It was often his job to go to a local restaurant for prepared food which his mother took home for a late evening supper for her family. Very often the family ate in a restaurant. One of Richard Peter's quiet observations about himself is that he has eaten out as often as at home. Dining out remains one of his favorite recreations.

The Hoffmans joined Trinity Reformed Church on Linden Street between Eleventh and Twelfth Streets. Richard Peter attended Sunday school and was confirmed there. His father served for many years as treasurer of the congregation, although Richard Peter actually kept the records when his father became involved in business activities which took him away from the store and house for long hours.

The lifestyle of the Hoffman family was similar to that of middle and upper-middle class Allentown families of Pennsylvania German background during these years. These Allentonians wanted to be assimilated into the dominant English-speaking culture of the nation. They worked successfully to achieve this goal. The most important step taken in this direction was to surrender use of the Pennsylvania German dialect. Both parents knew the dialect. Richard Peter remembers that they used it at home when he was a little boy. Suddenly, so he recalls, this ended. Still, it was spoken by everyone when his parents visited his Hoffman grandparents in rural Lehigh County. But it was not spoken in the Wotring home where grandfather had been a teacher of a one-room country school before he became a businessman. Thus, Richard Peter grew up with considerable exposure to the dialect. He never learned to speak it, though he can still understand many words and phrases and plays dialect vocabulary games with a friend. Incidentally, Grandfather Wotring had a strong influence upon his daughter, Stella. He was her teacher during the six years she spent in elementary school.

In addition to their involvement with their stores and their church, the parents also attended theater performances in Allentown and Philadelphia. Their home was a comfortable three-story, eight room with bath row house. The first floor was completely remodeled in 1948 and furnished with modernistic furniture selected by Richard Peter. The Hoffmans fitted well into Allentown which was profoundly Pennsylvania German, middle class, white and Protestant in its basic characteristics. It was also prosperous, growing and progressive in spirit. These people valued highly stable family life, regular religious observance, a strong work ethic, disciplined patterns of activity and cleanliness of person, home and neighborhood. Prior to World War II, Allentonians took pride in their city's reputation as "the Clean City" as much as in its reputation as a manufacturing and retail center. Richard Peter's way of life strongly reflected these values.

Richard Peter attended Allentown public schools—Franklin Elementary School, Central Junior High School and Allentown High School. In sixth grade, his teacher recognized his artistic talent and had him drawing posters on cardboard throughout the year. His academic ability enabled him to complete the three-year junior high school program in two years. At Allentown High School, he completed the academic course and graduated on June 27, 1927. His most memorable experiences were in the art courses offered by the high school which were taught by Anna Schadt. She made a small studio available to her students where they could work on their own.

In his senior year, Walter Emerson Baum was beginning his art lessons, which were offered on Saturday to select students, in Allentown. However, Richard Peter could not take advantage of this opportunity because, by this time, he was working every Saturday in his father's store. Richard Peter was afforded an important opportunity at self-growth and self-realization by Allentown High School in the art studio of Anna Schadt. He completed his course of study with a good academic record. Although he had participated in some extracurricular activities, he was still painfully shy.

Hoffman's parents were ambitious for their son. They hoped that he would enter one of the learned professions — law or medicine. They were aware of his interest in art and sought to discourage him from wasting his time and energy in a line of work which promised little in the way of financial security. Therefore, they accepted the suggestion of a friend, Lewis Acker, that Richard be sent to Mercersburg Academy to prepare for admission to Princeton University. Richard began a two-year program at Mercersburg in September 1927.

At that time, Mercersburg, affiliated with the Reformed Church, was one of the leading preparatory schools in the nation.

It attracted students from many states and several foreign countries. Almost all of its graduates were accepted at prominent colleges and universities. When Richard arrived at Mercersburg, he was very quiet and reserved, but not homesick. He made friends with another shy student, James Stewart, of Indiana, Pennsylvania. Stewart went on to Princeton and to Hollywood where he became the motion picture star, Jimmy Stewart.

In their senior year, Stewart and Hoffman produced the original drawings which illustrated the school yearbook, *The Karux*. These were done in the art deco style. Richard Peter took the only drawing course offered at Mercersburg, which was mechanical drawing taught by Dr. Lucien Clark Bareham. Bareham saw the interest of Hoffman and Stewart in drawing and set up a small, private class in which they prepared the drawings for *The Karux*. Two of his other professors, Archibald H. Rutledge and Frank Ellis Currier, encouraged him to take up art as a profession. Rutledge also permitted him to illustrate his English essays with drawings. Incidentally, he and Stewart were also members of the drama club, The Stoney Batter Club, and Richard acted in two plays. Richard Peter was also a member of the Glee Club, Choir and literary society.

In his second year at Mercersburg, his future became the subject of a family council held at the Hoffman homestead near Neffs. Richard wanted to go to art school, his parents still wanted him to apply to Princeton with law or medical school as the ultimate goal. Finally his paternal grandmother, Amanda Hoffman, ended the discussion by saying, "Lass das Kind sei," (Let the child be, let him do what he wants). Mercersburg had succeeded in changing Richard Peter; he had developed the courage and will to articulate his hopes and

From student days at Parsons:
Left: *Vanity Fair cover*
Below: *Two pen and ink drawings*

dreams for his future to his parents and family. Hopefully his parents appreciated this growth.

In September 1929, Hoffman entered the New York School of Fine and Applied Art, also known as Parsons School of Design, in New York City. This school had been recommended to him by both Anna Schadt and Lucien Clark Bareham. At that time it was located at 79th and Broadway and William M. Odom was its president. It was a leader among institutions preparing commercial artists. Richard completed its three-year program receiving a diploma in commercial art in 1932 with a major in Graphic Advertising and Decorative Illustration. He also took courses in interior architecture and decoration and costume design and illustration.

Even though Richard arrived in New York City just before the Great Stock Market Crash and remained there during the depth of the Great Depression, he found the city to be an exciting and stimulating place. The Chrysler Building had just been completed and the Empire State Building and Rockefeller Center were under construction. He frequently visited the Metropolitan Museum of Art and he attended the opening of the Museum of Modern Art. This museum opened a new world for him, and he became a charter member. He remains a member to this day. His interest in the theater grew rapidly. Even in 1932, there were more than two hundred openings on Broadway. Parsons students received passes to attend many of the shows to prepare sketches of sets, cast members and people in the audience. Hoffman saw the last Ziegfeld's *Follies* and Earl Carroll's *Vanities*. Parsons encouraged a close interaction of its students with the world of work. Leaders in the commercial art world came to the campus to lecture and to critique the work of the students. Richard completed an internship in window decoration at Bloomingdale's department store. In February 1932, a poster which he prepared won a prize at the Motion Picture Club Ball, which was held at the Waldorf-Astoria. His work at Parsons came to a climax when he was employed as an assistant instructor in Graphic Advertising and Illustration for the 1932 summer session. His plan of full-time employment in the fall term was thwarted when the college administration had to reduce its staff because of a decline in enrollment.

Hoffman found a job immediately at Stern's Department Store, located, at that time, on 42nd Street near Fifth Avenue. He worked there for about fourteen months, until November 1933, designing window displays before he was laid off. Through the final weeks of 1933 he worked as a free lance artist designing greeting cards and playing cards. While he sold a number of his works, the future was not promising, and he returned home early in 1934 to work in the grocery store and live with his parents at 1345 Turner Street.

Hoffman's Market at Tenth and Turner Streets in Allentown was not an ordinary corner grocery store serving a limited neighborhood clientele. It was a corner grocery store and it did serve its neighborhood. But George Moses Hoffman was an aggressive, innovative merchant who succeeded in building a store with a citywide reputation for selection, service, price and quality. The depression did not limit the growth of Hoffman's Market. By 1940, ten full-time people and two part-time people were employed there, including George Moses and Richard Peter, who worked full-time, and Stella, who worked part-time on Friday and Saturday taking telephone orders. One full-time and two part-time butchers served the meat department. Two vehicles

Store Personnel, ca. 1935. Front, left to right: George Moses Hoffman, Paul Hoffman, Mr. Guinther. Rear: Ralph Weidner, Eugene Sterner

delivered orders. To increase sales during the depression, two men went door-to-door in East Allentown taking orders for delivery. The store specialized in foods that tickled the palate of Pennsylvania Germans such as country-style meats prepared by a New Tripoli butcher and homemade baked goods, such as raised cakes prepared by an Allentown couple. Usually thirty or forty customers who had gone to the Farmer's Market at about 4:00 a.m. to buy produce were waiting for the 6:00 a.m. opening of the grocery store on Saturday morning. Hoffman's was the first store in Allentown to have frozen foods and to solicit new customers through the Welcome Wagon. The store was open from 7:00 a.m. to 5:30 p.m., Monday through Friday, and 6:00 a.m. to 6:00 p.m. on

Saturday. Customers could call in their orders which would be delivered to their homes; credit was available. George Moses believed in operating a clean, neat store with the most modern equipment. The walk-in refrigerator was washed every Monday morning; the asphalt tile placed on the floor as part of a thorough renovation in 1940 was shellacked by father and son, working on hands and knees, every six weeks.

Richard worked in the store for twenty-three years until it was sold by his father in 1957. It was the center of his life. In his first years of employment, he was one of his father's employees. But as time passed and his father had to spend more time out of the store, he became, in effect, the assistant manager with responsibility for all phases of the operation with the exception of the meat department. He became a reliable, efficient, knowledgeable grocer.

George Moses Hoffman not only operated a successful, independent grocery in Allentown, he was also a leader in the struggle for survival of the independent grocers in their competition with national grocery chains. He helped organize and served as president of the Lehigh Wholesale Grocery Company for thirty-three years. This was a firm which bought groceries in bulk at reduced prices for distribution to its member "Economy" stores. These were small, neighborhood independents scattered throughout eastern Pennsylvania. At one time more than three hundred grocers were members. It developed its own brand name, Trexler Park, for canned and packaged goods. In addition, George Moses was president of the Pennsylvania Retail Grocers Association for seven years, president of the Food Industry Associates of Allentown, vice president of the Retailers Mutual Insurance Company and a director of the Allentown Chamber of Commerce. He was on the board of the Second National Bank and, after its merger with First National, on the board of that bank. He was very active serving on the committee which assessed properties offered as security for loans. Later in his life, he was elected president of the board of the Phoebe-Devitt Home in Allentown, an agency of the Evangelical and Reformed Church serving the elderly. Beyond this, he was an active Mason and churchman.

Obviously, Richard's father was a very capable, hard working, committed man who made valuable contributions to his industry, church and community. It is also clear that he could not have carried those responsibilities without the quiet, efficient and, possibly, sacrificial support of his son.

Hoffman's Market, ca. 1915

At this point, a few comments may be in order about the relationship between father and mother and son. As one looks at family photographs, parents and son appear to be very happy with their lives and with each other. However, Richard feels that his parents controlled his life too rigorously. Both parents willingly committed their lives to the retail food industry. They worked hard in and for the store. They expected Richard Peter to do the same, and he complied. But there was a basic difference between him and his parents, particularly his father. The father devoted his life to work that was his first choice. Richard had to divide his life between his father's work and his art. There are many viable reasons why Richard stayed working at the store, even though his father did not require him to do so. Perhaps he remained because of loyalty to father and mother, knowing that his contribution was needed for the survival of the family enterprise. Part of the reason may have been because the store would be his when his father retired and the estate would be his upon the death of both parents. Maybe he stayed because his two major efforts to break into the art world were unsuccessful and he found a way of doing his art while remaining a full-time merchant. Ideally his parents might have been more understanding of the place of art in life. But there was little in their own experience to help them to see this connection. They did support him as fully as they could. They paid for his three years at Parsons, they placed no barrier to his extra-curricular art work after his return to Allentown, they attended his openings and they were proud of his window displays at the store.

Unfortunately, they did not understand abstract art. Stella chided Richard Peter for not painting pretty pictures. Even more unfortunately, they could not show their love by touching and embracing. Today, Richard is a happy man as he reviews his life and as he evaluates his present situation. He knows that his parents loved him, as he loved them. In addition, he admires his father for his achievements in the business world and community activities. He admires his mother as a homemaker, a business woman in her own right and as a virtual partner in the store. Their presence can still be felt in his home.

Upon his return to Allentown in 1934, Richard Peter soon developed a living pattern which enabled him to continue his interest in art. The working day was devoted to the store. Even here he found an outlet for his creativity in the window displays which he prepared on a weekly basis and which gained a growing and appreciative audience. But evenings and Sundays (after Sunday morning worship service) were his to devote to art.

He made two friends who supported and encouraged him in the years from 1934 to 1945. The one friend was William Swallow, a young art teacher of South Whitehall High School, who lived in Allentown at 1346 Linden Street, one block from the Hoffmans at 1345 Turner Street. Richard Peter and William soon became good friends. Richard Peter spent a great deal of time in the Swallow home and even considered moving in with him. They were both about the same age and had a burning passion for art. Swallow's forte was ceramic sculpture, and he rapidly gained a regional reputation for his creations which emphasized Pennsylvania German subjects. Stimulated by Swallow, Hoffman tried his hand at ceramics and produced several promising works, but his strength was in painting and he did not pursue ceramics beyond the experimental level. The other friend was Betty Davis, who had attended Parsons at the same time as Richard Peter, though they had not known each other there. She came to

Top: Nestle's Window Exhibit, ca. 1945
Middle: William Swallow Window Exhibit, ca. 1950
Bottom: Ceramics

Allentown with her parents during World War II. At her invitation, a group of local amateur artists made her home, near Eleventh and Hamilton Streets, a studio. In this circle, Richard Peter worked in water colors, building on a class in that medium, which he had taken at Parsons. Briefly, in 1937-38, Richard Peter gave art lessons to three students in his own third-floor studio on Turner Street.

In 1937, Professor Garth Howland, chairman of the Lehigh University Art Department, organized the Lehigh Art Alliance. Richard Peter was one of the charter members of this organization. When it began, the Alliance had about thirty members; today it has about three hundred members. The Alliance soon developed a pattern of conducting two business meetings and holding two major exhibitions each year. Richard Peter also designed stage sets for local theatrical shows. As the 1930s came to an end, Richard Peter also developed an interest in photography. One of his works won an award from the New York World's Fair in 1939. In recognition of his growth, the Allentown Art Museum displayed his water colors and photographs in 1940. Thus, by the end of the decade, Richard Peter was active as an amateur artist, photographer and ceramicist. But he was still searching for the medium, subject matter and form on which he could concentrate his talent.

In September 1939, World War II began. At first it was a European war, involving primarily Great Britain, France and Germany. The United States did not become involved, as a belligerent, until December 1941. In 1939, the American people found their country woefully unprepared. Among other measures, Congress enacted a draft law, which took effect late in 1940. In the spring of 1941, as a single man of thirty without dependents, Richard Peter was called for induction into military service. While he passed a preliminary physical in Allentown, he failed the physical examination in Wilkes-Barre and was classified 4-F. He remained at home, working in the store during the war years. When rationing was begun, he was given the responsibility of keeping track of the coupons customers turned in for various groceries and meats. In the evenings he painted occasionally with Betty Davis and members of the Art Alliance. But he found no joy in this work. Free-flowing water colors had become meaningless to him.

The war ended in the late summer of 1945. For millions of former servicemen and their wives and sweethearts, the winter of 1945-46 meant the beginning of a new life. This period was also a time of new beginnings for Richard Peter, but for other reasons. Late in 1945, his parents were involved in an automobile accident. While not injured permanently, they required some time for recuperation. During this period, Richard Peter had the full responsibility for management of the store. Added to this pressure was the suppressed longing for a career as a professional artist. These pressures brought him close to a nervous breakdown. In his confusion, he sought guidance from a local psychiatrist who recommended that he take one day a week for painting and that he continue his theater activities.

Consequently, in 1946 Richard Peter made major decisions which controlled his artistic activity from that year until 1967. He decided upon painting in a variant of the abstract style using water color, tempera and crayon. He also decided upon a uniform size of the paper he would employ and the type of frame in which the completed work would be placed. Among the subjects he decided upon were symbols from the Pennsylvania German cultural experience. He was encouraged to move in this direction by Bill Swallow, by the ethnic background of his family and by the flowering of Pennsylvania German heritage studies and activities which began in the mid-1930s and of which Allentown was a leading center. This movement toward the abstract was a significant change for Richard Peter for, up to that point in his career, his emphasis had been upon living subjects taken from nature.

Another important resource, which he cultivated from 1946 on, was his friendship with Verna Ruth. Verna, an English teacher at Central Junior High School in Allentown, understood modern art. She quickly became a trusted and reliable counselor. When Richard Peter reached an impasse in creating a work, he called upon Ruth for advice, and, invariably, she suggested a solution to the problem. She also served as his secretary and press agent and assisted him in preparing exhibits of his work in museums. Along with Bill Swallow, she became the major influence in his artistic life. A third friend was Edgar T. Clewell, a professional photographer who prepared photographs of Richard Peter's work. A fourth friend was another English teacher, Ruth Roth, who was on the faculty of Allentown High School.

The first major exhibition of Richard Peter's abstracts was held at the Henry Salpeter Gallery, located on East 56th Street in New York City, from April 19 to May 8, 1948. At that time, Henry Salpeter was the Fine Arts Editor of *Esquire* magazine. His gallery was devoted to the work of promising young American artists. Richard Peter had been directed to him by a friend in the Lehigh Art Alliance. This exhibit consisted of seventeen water colors dealing with Pennsylvania German subjects. The brochure described Richard Peter and his work in these terms:

> This is the first New York exhibition of Richard Peter Hoffman of Allentown, Pa., a member of a Pennsylvania Dutch family which came to this country eight generations ago. Most of his paintings, executed in a combination of water color and crayon, constitute a modern interpretation of and variations upon the traditional folk art of rural Pennsylvania, the work of artisans whose craft was a daily celebration of a simple, ordered existence in which full value was given to the virtues of thrift, cleanliness, honesty, health and fruitfulness.

In commenting upon Hoffman's work, a critic in *The New York Times* stated:

> Art with strong Pennsylvania Dutch roots that disciplines feeling with design: Respect for simplicity in life, farm, church, home. Source of stability welcome in midst of current art neuroses.

Although this and other reviews were favorable, Richard Peter did not sell a single painting. However, *Fortune magazine* photographed each painting for possible future use. *Fortune* also engaged him to prepare a Christmas edition cover. While Richard Peter was paid for this work, it was never published. His first effort to break into the New York art world had failed.

In these years, articles describing and evaluating Hoffman's work, particularly the pieces reflecting his Pennsylvania German heritage, appeared in several periodicals. One, written by Verna Ruth, was published in the *Pennsylvania Dutchman* of June 1, 1950. In it, Hoffman defined his work in these terms:

> My paintings are purely decorative in design . . . I am interested only in creating pleasing lines, textures and color combinations. Whatever others may see in my paintings, they read into them from their own experience with the familiar Dutch symbols. As our great-grandfathers used hearts, flowers, stars and birds as the stylistic form of their age, so an artist

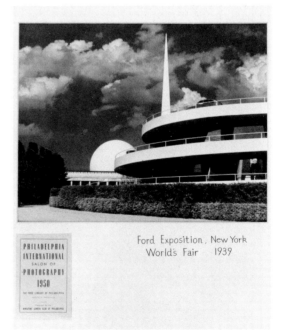

Ford Exposition, New York
World's Fair   1939

PHILADELPHIA
INTERNATIONAL
SALON OF
PHOTOGRAPHY
1950

today may interpret these same motifs in modern abstract form. The motifs remain the same, but the manner of treatment differs with the age. The *Pennsylvania Dutchman* may be conservative, but he can also be alert to the trend of his time.

Ruth described his method in these words:

> Using a combination of water color, tempera and crayon, Hoffman has experimented with new techniques in his chosen medium. This is primarily the aim in all his paintings. For that reason he occasionally leaves his Dutch subjects and portrays scenes with almost photographic realism or paints marine and nature studies with his characteristic precision. He believes that the field of water color painting has unlimited possibilities for exploration and experimentation.

By the summer of 1950, after little more than three years of intense effort, Richard Peter had amassed important credentials. In addition to membership in the Lehigh Art Alliance, he was also a member of the Philadelphia Water Color Club and the Woodmere Art Gallery. He was a member of the board of directors of the Lehigh Art Alliance. His paintings had been exhibited widely in National Water Color shows and Audubon Artists shows in New York City; by the Philadelphia Art Alliance, the Pennsylvania Academy of Fine Arts, the Woodmere Art Gallery in Philadelphia and the Gimbel Art Gallery in New York; in New Hope, Reading, Bethlehem and Allentown and in local college art galleries. In addition, he had his one-man show in the Salpeter Gallery in New York City. He was completely at home with the abstract style. He experienced a new life filled with discovery and fueled by an outburst of energy which enabled him to carry a heavy work load at the store and in his studio.

Another of Richard Peter's friends was Olive Zehner of Reading, who was among the leaders of the Kutztown, Pennsylvania

Dutch Folk Festival. In 1954, Zehner was asked by the producers to assist in casting their projected musical about the Pennsylvania Dutch, *Plain and Fancy*. In turn, Olive invited Richard Peter to work with her. He accepted and was involved in planning the production. He was invited to and attended the opening night party in January 1955. This led to his second one-man art show which was arranged by Dick Colmar, another New York City art critic. This exhibit was held at Gimbel's Department Store to coincide with the opening of *Plain and Fancy*. However, as in 1948, he failed to sell a single painting. Later that same year, he had an interview with Dan Cooper, a leading New York City textile designer, who had expressed strong interest in his work. However, this interview did not result in a job offer because of personality differences between the two men. Nineteen fifty-five was the year of Hoffman's second major effort to find a full-time base for his art in New York City. The effort failed, and he did not try again.

Still he enjoyed a real measure of local and regional acceptance. Richard Hirsch, director of the Allentown Art Museum, presented an exhibition of 27 of his paintings from February 25-March 18, 1962. In his introduction to Hoffman's work, Hirsch wrote:

> His (Hoffman's) roots in Pennsylvania provide the life-blood of virtually all of his paintings. He consciously identifies himself and his art with these roots in an ancestral soil. The traditions of design of Pennsylvania folk-art, most often, are the ignition sparks for his inspiration.
>
> Hoffman is immersed in tradition. He seeks out the traditional forms and brings them to us, revealed by a singular metamorphosis.

A year later, from February 10-March 3, 1963, Edith Emerson, director of The Woodmere Art Gallery in Philadelphia, also presented an exhibit of Richard Peter's work consisting of 44 of his watercolors.

As the years passed, major changes took place in Richard Peter's living pattern. One basic change occurred in 1953 when his parents sold their home at 1345 Turner Street and moved to a newly constructed brick rancher at 1035 North Thirtieth Street in Allentown's upper-middle class northwestern suburb. This attractive home with living space concentrated on one floor undoubtedly appealed to his aging parents. Richard Peter chose modernistic furniture for the new family home. Another basic change occurred in 1957 when the store was sold. For several years prior to the sale, father, mother and son had agreed to continue the ownership and operation on a year-to-year basis. All were aware of the heavy burden the store was placing upon the father as he was growing older and was becoming ever more deeply involved in community activities. All were aware that Richard Peter did not plan to assume sole management of the store. It was more and more difficult to find reliable part-time help. Finally, one Saturday, George Moses had to drive the delivery truck. This was the last straw for Richard Peter. That evening, in a family council, the decision was made to sell the store to a cousin, Paul Hoffman, who was in charge of the meat department. Within two weeks, the deal was completed, and George Moses and Richard Peter no longer had to make the early morning commute, Monday through Saturday, from home to store. With their departure the store changed—not in appearance but in the style, vigor and resourcefulness of its management. George Moses was now free to give his full time to his retirement activities which included service on the board of the First National Bank of Allentown and presidency of the board of the Phoebe-Devitt Home. Richard Peter found a new job in 1958 as a teller at the Nineteenth Street Branch of First National. Before his retirement from that position in 1968, he had advanced to the position of chief teller.

During all those years he continued to paint and to exhibit in his spare time. However, his productivity declined appreciably from 1960 onward. His creative flame was beginning to wane. He suffered a severe emotional loss in 1964 with the death of his father. This followed closely upon the death of William Swallow in 1962; Edgar T. Clewell died in 1965, and Verna Ruth, in tragic circumstances, in 1967. Nineteen sixty-eight became a year of decision. In order to care for his mother, Richard Peter retired from his bank job, and decided to give up painting completely.

Still, his days were busy. He chose color photography as his channel of artistic expression. This was not a new departure for him. He had used the camera for many years as an adjunct to his painting. Now he used photography as the medium to explore, understand and interpret form in the natural and manmade world. Again,

Richard, Stella and George Hoffman, May 1950

as in painting, he turned to the landscape of Lehigh County which was filled with Pennsylvania German symbolism. He produced a series of color photographs on the "Four Seasons in Lehigh County." He had these reproduced as color slides which he presented in an illustrated lecture to many civic and church organizations. Richard Peter found a capable associate in Mrs. Eleanore Bentz, an Allentown commercial photographer, who developed, enlarged and printed his negatives. Bryan Caldwell, the director of the Allentown Art Museum, encouraged him. He exhibited his photographs at the Allentown Art Museum in 1972 and at the First National Bank in 1972 and 1975. A reviewer for the *Call-Chronicle* summarized his reactions to the latter show in these words:

> It is a stunning show and fascinating at every glance. For Hoffman, snow and light become fantastic miracles, light and shadow are alive with meanings, patterns have moods…pure geometrics have emotions. Actually, anyone who knows Hoffman's paintings knows how the artist's mind works in passions and in detail, precisely ordered with calipers or a draftsman's compass. That feeling for what might be called the flatland of lines of reduction to abstraction of essence permeates the camera-holder's vision as well.

In recent years his photographs have been displayed at the Mountain House on Lake Mohonk, near New Paltz, New York. His portfolio contains more than 200 photographs.

If painting and photography were the first passions of Hoffman's life, his second was the theater. An inveterate theater-goer throughout his life, Richard Peter in 1966 organized a theatre night for his fellow members of the Allentown West End Kiwanis Club. The success of this venture led him to form a local theater club whose bus excursions to plays, musicals and opera in New York City, Philadelphia, New Hope and many other locations became legendary in the Lehigh Valley. Over 18 years, he conducted 355 tours for a club whose total membership reached 3,007.

He attended one of the first productions of the Bucks County Playhouse shortly after it opened in 1939. In 1940 he became a subscriber and remains one to this day. As the 1989 season ended and as the Playhouse celebrated its 50th anniversary, Richard Peter attended his 496th presentation. Among his special memories is the first-ever performance of Grace Kelly. The Playhouse management recognized his attendance at both his 350th and 400th shows. He is anticipating his 500th show early in the 1990 season.

He has also supported strongly the Civic Little Theatre in Allentown. He has attended all but two of its presentations since it was organized in 1934. He served as its historian from 1934 until 1976, keeping a file of the programs and newspaper publicity for every show.

He became the historian of the Pennsylvania Stage Company from 1979, when it was organized, until the present. He has seen every one of its productions and has been a generous financial supporter of this enterprise. He has also served as the historian of the Allentown Community Concert Association for the past 18 years. He made a financial contribution which made it possible for his church, First Presbyterian, which he joined in 1979, to build a stage in its new parish center. He also serves as historian of the Lehigh Art Alliance. His collection of programs, newspaper clippings and personal diaries is an invaluable resource for future students of the cultural life of Allentown and the Lehigh Valley. His support of the Theater led the *Sunday Call-Chronicle* to name Richard Peter "Allentown's Mr. Theater" in 1984.

Delivery Van, ca. 1925

In 1978 Hoffman had the large basement of his home converted into an attractive and serviceable museum and conference center. He took the first steps to will the house and its contents—his paintings, photographs and collections of roosters and Pennsylvania German folk art—to the County of Lehigh. This facility is used as a conference center by county officials and civic groups.

In 1973, Richard Peter's mother died at the age of 90 while a guest at the Phoebe Home. During her illness, he visited her every day.

Two of Richard Peter's hobbies reveal the man. His home is filled with his collection of roosters which was begun more than 50 years ago. They add a bright, even a flamboyant, note to the interior of 1035 North Thirtieth. They represent a wide variety of shapes, materials, colors and sizes. In a real way they reflect his lifelong concern for difference within unity. Eighteen years ago he encouraged a number of his friends, men and women, to meet each Monday morning for breakfast, either in a restaurant or in one of their homes. The group is still largely intact and is still meeting regularly. Companionship expressed in a warm body of friends partaking of a simple meal on a regular basis is a meaningful part of Hoffman's life. Finally, there is his collection of diaries and statistics which provide a minutely accurate summary of his many varied activities. His achievements in the arts have led to his inclusion in *Who's Who in the East, Who's Who in American Art, Dictionary of International Biography* and *Artists/USA*.

Struggle in Richard Peter's life was not a battle for survival against external forces such as economic depression or world war. The store produced income sufficient for him to complete his course at Parsons during the depth of depression. Physical disabilities kept him from military service during the Second World War—a service he was willing to undertake. Struggle in his life meant establishing his identity as an artist, and a competent grocer, and in developing a satisfying relationship with his father and mother. Several years ago, in a newspaper interview, Richard Peter summarized his life:

> I've managed to have a lot of fun with my life...I'm certainly glad I came back from that New York.

Today, Richard Peter Hoffman is, as he always has been, a precise, busy, well-organized, yet kind, gentle, generous, compassionate man who has found meaning for his life in his paintings, photography, home, family and friends. He remains a thriving old bachelor without a woman behind him.

1. Five Pines Farm **May 1946**
A representational water color typical of
Hoffman's work from the 1930s to May 1946.
The farm is near Guthsville, Pennsylvania.

RICHARD PETER
HOFFMAN

Pennsylvania German Precisionist
by Scott T. Swank

RICHARD PETER HOFFMAN SET OFF IN THE FALL OF 1929 FOR THE HEADY URBAN ENVIRONMENT OF NEW YORK CITY TO STUDY COMMERCIAL art at The New York School of Fine and Applied Art, commonly known as The Parsons School of Design. Within a few months Hoffman had moved from the hallowed, traditional and bucolic atmosphere of Mercersburg Academy, with its Gothic chapel, to the cosmopolitan and frantic life of New York, the center of world finance and art, where he witnessed the Great Crash of 1929, the opening of the Museum of Modern Art, and the building of Rockefeller Center. Of all these events, the one Hoffman remembers most vividly is the opening of MOMA. There the art, so wild, colorful and different from anything he had ever seen, made New York City seem tame by comparison.

New York, 1929-1933

Parsons was a logical choice for Hoffman. Anna Schadt, his high school art teacher, was a Parsons graduate. Dr. Bareham, his professor of drawing at Mercersburg and a Cornell University graduate, also recommended Parsons. With Hoffman's drawing skills already well developed, the Parsons program in graphic advertising and illustration promised a way to harness artistic talent to a practical career. Although New York was an alien place for a shy young man from Pennsylvania, Hoffman thrived. At Parsons he sat for lectures, but the bulk of his work was drawing and painting, moving through a carefully choreographed program of classes in color theory and drawing. Figural drawing was done from live nude models, in-class exercises and on visits to museums. Artists and commercial designers came to Parsons to criticize and review student work. Students were assigned practical problems, for example to design a greeting card, create a poster, plan a department store window layout for Bloomingdale's, or attack a design problem presented by *Good Housekeeping*. Students were encouraged to explore the museums and cityscape of New York (boats, department stores, rooftops) for design ideas. Hoffman consistently received the highest marks of "excellent" in graphic design.

Hoffman graduated from the New York School of Fine and Applied Art in June, 1932. His work in the Graphic Advertising and Illustration course won a scholarship from Parsons for "creative ability and originality in design."[1] He was asked to join the faculty as an assistant instructor for the Department of Graphic Advertising and Illustration. However, after the summer school ended Hoffman was informed that funds were not available to keep him employed at Parsons. Hoffman took his art portfolio into the streets of New York in 1932 in the midst of the Great Depression.

During the fall Hoffman survived on the work of his pen and his strong sense of design. He was hired on a weekly basis to create store window displays for Sterns ($25.00 per week). As a freelance designer he supplemented his income with greeting card designs which he marketed (generally at $5.00 per design) to Norcross and Brownie's Blockprint, Inc. Over the course of 18 months Hoffman designed 93 Christmas cards and sold 57 of them. He also designed birthday and bon voyage cards and even some playing cards. Nevertheless, as the hold of the depression deepened in the winter of 1933 and spring of 1934, Hoffman's employment record shows that his income slowed to a trickle until it ceased in the winter of 1934. Discouraged, Hoffman decided to return home.

2. Country Forms   ***May 1946***
Just as the title shifted from a specific farm to "country forms," so too the essence of the landscape was abstracted into geometric shapes and free-flowing designs. The change in style was not deliberate, but "just happened" on the spot.

Allentown, 1934-1946

Home was 1345 Turner Street in Allentown, his childhood residence. Employment was waiting at his father's grocery store at nearby 10th and Turner Street, where Hoffman worked long hours six days a week. At first he had no interest in continuing his painting, although he did enter completed works in local art shows. Gradually he began creating window displays for the grocery store. By late 1934 he returned to painting and his work gained local and ultimately national recognition with his inclusion in the 1935 edition of *Who's Who in American Art*.

By the late 1930s Hoffman was fully engaged in the local and regional art scene, which extended to New York and Philadelphia. He painted regularly with

6. Taufschein Bird   June 1946
The bird model for this painting was a pair of ceramic lovebirds facing each other which was sculpted by Hoffman in Bill Swallow's studio. A taufschein is a document used by Reformed and Lutheran churches to record and commemorate the birth and baptism of children.

5. Pennsylvania Dutch Designs   June 1946
Hoffman's first Pennsylvania Dutch Watercolor uses traditional motifs such as birds, hearts and tulips in an original composition with non-traditional colors of green and brown. The mixture of traditional motifs and modernist design becomes a hallmark of his work.

23

8. Pennsylvania Dutch Barn **July 1946**
*Once again the ceramic lovebird makes an
appearance, along with traditional inhabitants
of Pennsylvania barns, and a modern rendition
of a Lehigh County barn star.*

Betty Davis, a local artist with a studio on South 11th Street. Davis was the daughter of a designer who worked for the Veetol corporation. Once a week a small band of devotees gathered in her home studio to paint free-hand water colors. Hoffman enjoyed the companionship of like-minded people at these soirees. Hoffman was also active in the Lehigh Art Alliance, formed in 1937.

In 1937 Hoffman opened his own third-floor studio on Turner Street to students for art instruction. A total of three students over 1937-38 (Jane Schwartz, Charles Roth and Charlotte Halliday) attended weekly or biweekly classes. Instruction stopped abruptly in 1938 because Hoffman felt he no longer had anything to teach them.

In addition to teaching, Hoffman also designed stage sets for local theatrical presentations and entered formal floral arrangements in local flower shows. He cultivated his photographic interests and by 1939 was proficient enough to win a photo contest at the New York World's Fair (see pg. 15). Ceramics was another medium that caught his attention, and in 1940 he began experimentation in the sculpture studio of William Swallow, a local teacher and personal friend.

In 1940 Hoffman's local esteem was recognized by a show at the Allentown Art Museum, where 17 of his watercolors were displayed in one gallery and 35 photographs in two additional galleries. The show was notable not only for recognizing the work of a contemporary local artist, but also because it marked a pioneer effort on the part of the museum. Hoffman's photographs constituted the first art photography exhibition at the Allentown Museum of Art.

During World War II Hoffman busied himself with a standard routine of work at his father's grocery. He also maintained a

15. Distelfink and Heart   *January 1947*
Hoffman's fascination with pattern is seen clearly. Inspiration was found in swatches of homespun linen from the Kohler house in Kutztown, Pennsylvania, one of the largest nineteenth century mansions in Kutztown. Hoffman's aunt had married a Kohler and was living in the Kutztown mansion in the 1940s.

16. Alley by Night   **March 1947**
The scene is the backyard of the Hoffman home at 1345 Turner Street in Allentown, a street of rowhouses with one car garages. In precisionist fashion, Hoffman dramatizes the contrasts and patterns of an ordinary urban street scene on a clear winter evening.

17. Pennsylvania Dutch   **March 1947**
    Cookie Cutters
Hoffman's first experiment with modernist collage features abstractions of tin cookie cutters, an essential tool in any Pennsylvania German woman's kitchen, and a background of actual recipes pasted to the surface. The painting of roosters in all forms mirrors a collecting interest of Hoffman. The line pattern reflects the "string" collage paintings of Bill Swallow, who created entire pictures with string.

schedule of cultural activities, mostly art and theater related. He continued to paint occasionally with Betty Davis and her studio group. He served on the board of the Lehigh Art Alliance and painted with its members. He also sculpted in the ceramic studio of Bill Swallow, a neighbor and friend who was an art teacher at what is now Troxell Junior High School, in South Whitehall Township. They had met through the newly formed Lehigh Art Alliance shortly after Hoffman's return from New York in 1933. Swallow, formally trained in Philadelphia, was Allentown's finest sculptor. In 1940 Hoffman learned to work in ceramics and created four pieces still in his personal collection (Angel - 1940; Hen - 1940; Amish Lady - 1941; Love Birds - unfired, 1941). Although Hoffman also created a few other ceramic works in the 1940s, his interest was transitory and largely based on the camaraderie he shared with Swallow.

Allentown, 1946

Hoffman's life and work took a dramatic turn in 1946, when a serious automobile accident nearly took the lives of his parents. The crisis that followed, however, was not one primarily with his parents but with himself, his future and his art.

In 1946 all of the tension of Hoffman's emotional crisis led him to seek the advice of a psychiatrist. Hoffman was strongly urged to spend one day a week painting, since painting seemed to be a satisfactory outlet for his emotions. Although painting was an expressive medium for Hoffman, it was also a source of frustration. His representational water colors did not fulfill his creative urge and left him feeling restricted. Under the new regimen of one day per week, Hoffman started anew with his work in May 1946. To his pleasant surprise, as he began to paint, his work underwent

19. Taufschein   **April 1947**
Pairs of birds, standing angels and trees of life
are all traditional designs for Pennsylvania
German birth and baptismal certificates.

24. Amish School Girl   **July 1947**

*In the 1940s the Old Order Amish were
"discovered" by National Geographic Magazine,
Broadway and post World War II tourism. Interest
in the dress and customs of the Amish was strong
within and outside their settlement area, and that
interest included artists such as Bill Swallow,
who featured the Amish in his ceramic sculpture.
The figure of the Amish girl in this painting is
derived from a specific Swallow work. The
transparent abstract designs include a tulip,
picket fencing and window panes of ABC blocks.*

a sudden and radical transformation, as illustrated in two paintings of the same landscape scene, both done in 1946 after the accident and after being advised to explore self-help art therapy (cf. pp. 20, 22).

From 1934 to 1946 Hoffman exhibited his representational water colors at local shows as well as in New York City, Philadelphia, and Wilmington, Delaware. Most of the pictures were landscapes—scenes sketched on Sunday afternoon travels into the countryside. Lesser numbers of works concentrated on architecture (farmhouses and barns), still lifes and other subjects. They are competently executed and Hoffman won some critical acclaim for this early work, but very few paintings sold. Actually, it was his very early work, done at Parsons and after his return to Allentown that led to his inclusion in the first edition in 1935 of *Who's Who in American Art*. That edition featured one of his water color still lifes entitled *Ivy, White*

Vase and Box, 1935. In 1935 he exhibited in a large water color show (1,000 pictures) at the Pennsylvania Academy of Fine Arts in Philadelphia, where one of his works was then selected (with 137 others) for an exhibit by the Wilmington Water Color Society (*Dancers*, 1935).[2] The quality of his work of this period is ably represented by *Portrait of a Negro Done Under Purple Lamp Light*, 1934, even though its specific subject—a black male—and portrait work generally, were not Hoffman's stock in trade.

All of these shows demonstrated Hoffman's considerable drawing skill, but his work showed no progression, and it was not characterized by a distinctive style. His painting revealed only a fragment of his

Left:

31. Apple Butter   February 1948

All the ingredients for tart, black-brown apple butter, a staple of Pennsylvania German eating, are represented here, including apples, a copper kettle, a wooden stirrer with tiny apples for holes, the recipe and a stoneware storage crock.

Right:

43. Gallery Studio   November 1948

Hoffman's circle of artist friends included Miss Jerry Quier of Bethlehem. Modernist artists, with their emphasis on individual creativity, were fascinated with each other's studios as well as their own. Quier's studio was located at 1522 Center Street in Bethlehem.

academic and practical training at Parsons in color and design. Consequently, the numerous landscapes and still lifes which dominate his work from 1935 through May 1946 seem static and lifeless.

The Development of a Style, 1946-1950

The crisis of 1946 altered Hoffman's perception of life, himself and his art. Like the rush of water from a broken dam, Hoffman's art from May 1946 begins to express his life experience and reflect the impact of Modernism on his life in those critical, formative years in New York from 1929-1933.

From May 1946 through 1950, Hoffman produced 54 water colors which in their range of subject, technique, color and design show that he was experimenting with self-imposed parameters that can be identified as a distinctive style. Within that style, Hoffman worked on several regular variations. For example, from May through December 1946, Hoffman created twelve

45. After the Storm   **January 1949**
The home of friends near the present day Valley Forge Music Fair.

paintings which were clearly unlike anything he had done previously. In subject matter and execution they vary considerably, but all remain within the framework of his "new" style.

During 1946 Hoffman touches on most of the subject themes to which he returns in his later work. The first new painting is a country landscape. Still lifes and buildings reappear in "modern renditions" of earlier work. But new themes also emerge, such as the Pennsylvania Dutch, circuses, seaside/beach subjects and a geometric abstraction! Subject matter is important to Hoffman in 1946, so the subject matter of most paintings in that year is identifiable but the entire premise of his art has shifted in 1946 from representation to modernism. Color, design and the creative process of the artist have, in true modernist fashion, overthrown the tyranny of subject matter. The observer is now forced to deal with the individual work of art on its own terms rather than judging it on the degree to which it is a faithful representation of the subject at hand.

During 1947, Hoffman settled comfortably within the aesthetic and philosophical framework of modernism, expressing Cubist thought in his practice of breaking subjects into geometric units and then reassembling

Continued on page 65

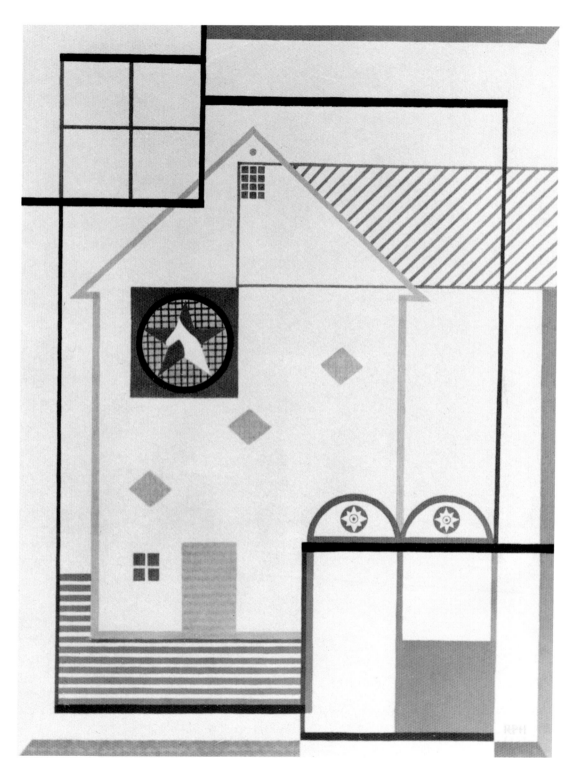

46. Barn Abstraction　　　　**February 1949**
Hoffman explored barn motifs frequently throughout his career, often accentuating their size and simple design elements with stunning effect.

48. Refreshers   **March 1949**
In this Precisionist work Hoffman, like Charles
Sheeler, draws inspiration from historic Colonial
Williamsburg. The painting is one of the first
in which Hoffman relies on his own black and
white photography.

Color
Paintings

Portrait of a Negro Done   **1934**
Under Purple Lamp Light

In subject matter, composition, color and emotion, this figural study is one of Hoffman's strongest works from the pre-1946 period.

9. Pink Lemonade   August 1946

Hoffman playfully combines his love of the circus with a masterful design.
He manipulates geometry by carefully balancing circles and triangles in a variety
of sizes to express, in timeless, semi-abstract form, the joy of life.

32. Quilt Applique   **February 1948**

This painting is one of Hoffman's most successful early efforts to express his Pennsylvania German heritage. It evokes a strong feeling for family life and traditional motifs in a multi-layered composition of exceptional three-dimensional quality.

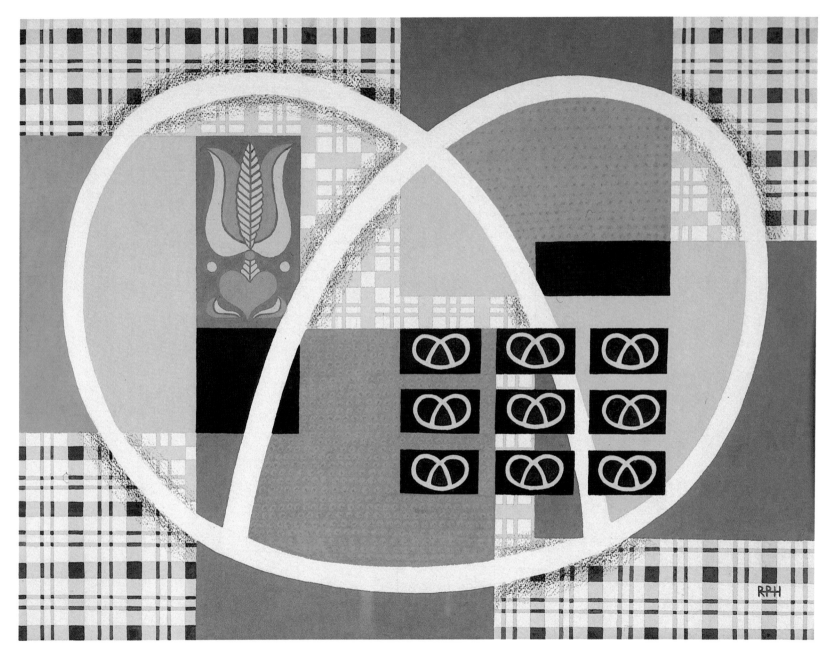

33. Pretzels   March 1948

Hoffman's modern "no twist" pretzels on a homespun plaid background once again address the comforting theme of Pennsylvania German home life. The design and color combination are very contemporary for the late 1940s.

37. The Swallow House   June 1948

*Sculptor Bill Swallow lived with his mother in this farmhouse near Allentown, with a
studio and "chicken coop" art gallery on the same property. Hoffman presents an
abstraction of the house and the tree in its front yard in Cubist style as a backdrop
to several of Swallow's sculptures and mobiles.*

40. Symbols In The Night   **August 1948**

Brilliant barn stars as flying saucers in a turbulent night make this one of Hoffman's most creative and powerful compositions. With no direct reference to any specific scene or subject, this image is one of the artist's most compelling "Modernist" works.

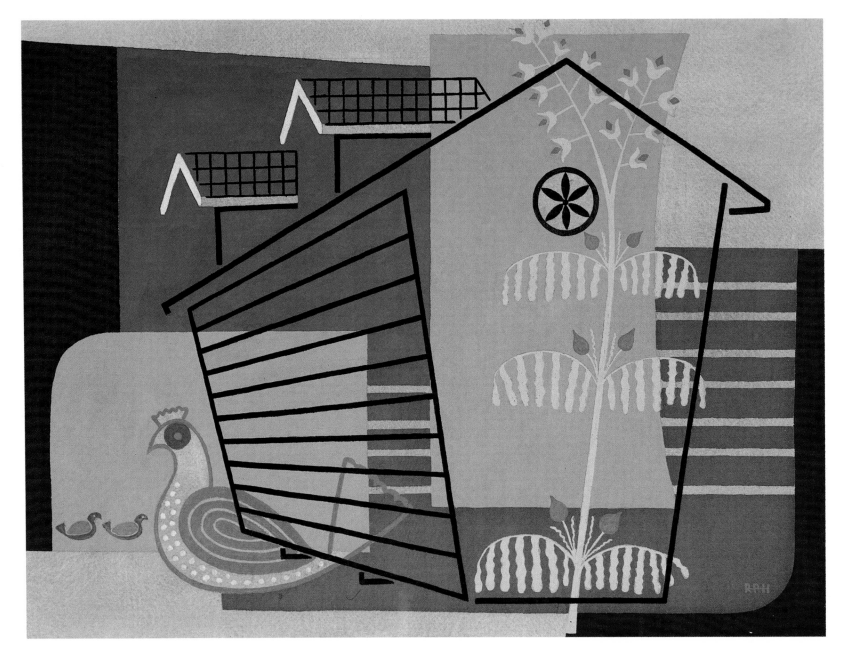

51. Corner of a Barnyard   **July 1949**

Through abstraction, Hoffman elevates the lowly corncrib to a symbol of bountiful harvests on the prosperous farms of Lehigh County. The soft colors and their mixture reflect the artist's Parsons training.

71. Pennsylvania Dutch Tombstones   **September 1950**

Done in India ink, the only example of Hoffman's work in this medium, this Cubist painting draws its inspiration from the cemetery of Heidelberg Union Church northwest of Allentown.

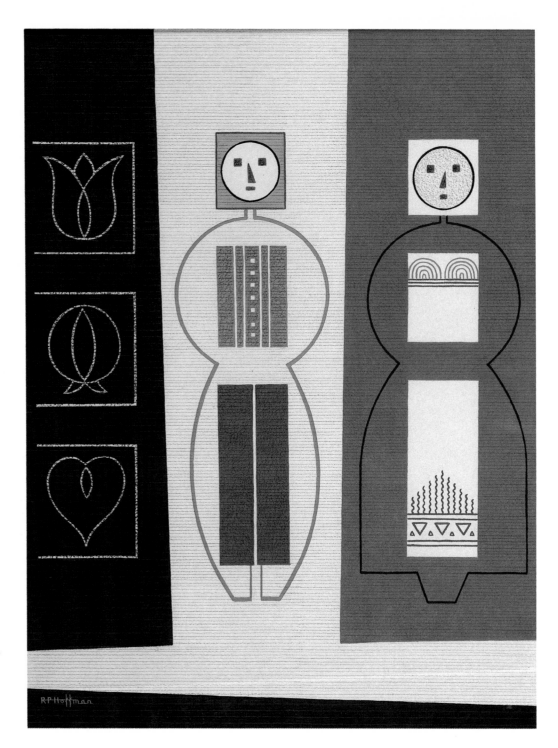

107. Pennsylvania Dutch   June 1954
Block Heads

*One suspects double meaning in Hoffman's playful
choice of title for this painting, which draws heavily
on Russian icons for its inspiration and on folk art
generally for its one-dimensional look.*

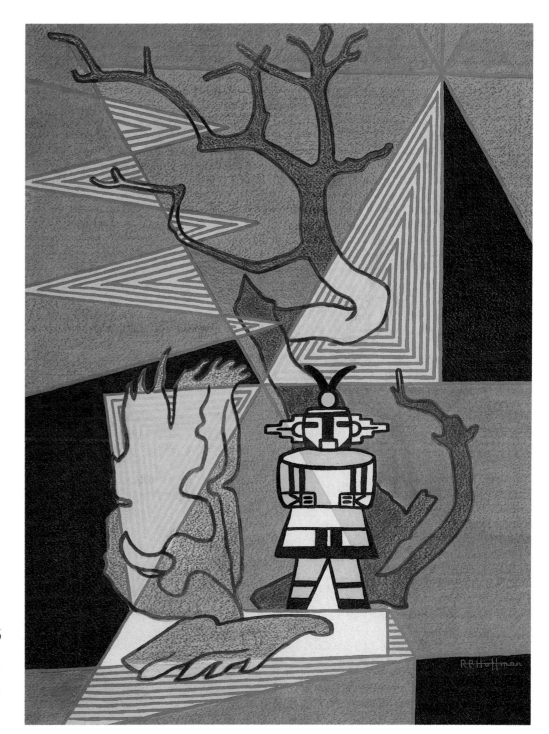

118. Primeval Days   January 1956

*New inspiration for the artist often came through
travel, and numerous paintings over the years compress
a trip into one or several images. In this case travel to
the Southwest emerges in a highly original Cubist work
where color, pattern and images are distinctively
Southwestern.*

126. Pennsylvania Dutch Summer House   **July 1956**

This spare but elegant image is one of Hoffman's finest Precisionist works in terms of composition, contrast and balance, comparing favorably to the precisionist works of Charles Sheeler and Georgia O'Keefe.

183. Studio Forms No. 2   **July 1962**

This Modernist rendering is one of a series of studio portraits which Hoffman executed over the years. In it we find his desk, bookshelf, plant, books and paintings abstracted and colorfully portrayed in a style reminiscent of Stuart Davis' work.

184. Good Morning   **June 1963**

Many of Hoffman's paintings, including this example, can best be classified as still lifes. In this excellent image the artist draws an antique coffee pot and tea pot from one of his favorite scources of inspiration — the kitchen.

Pennsylvania Dutch   **March 1963**
No. 188

There is a return to strong Pennsylvania German
images in the last year of Hoffman's painting, as is
reflected in this work which the artist alternately
named "Three Button Tulips."

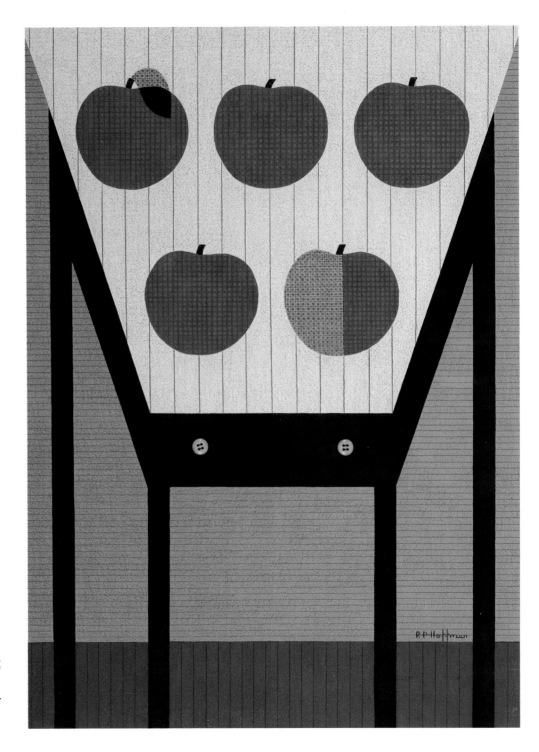

Pennsylvania Dutch   **May 1965**
No. 189

Hoffman's last painting is one of his strongest. Alternately titled "Five Apples," this painting is related to "White Top Table," June 1959.

Color
Photographs

1978, Fall Crocus
Kodak Ectachrome 64 Film
Konica 35 mm. camera
15″ x 20″

1979, The Rose
Kodak Ectachrome 64 Film
Konica 35 mm. camera
15" x 20"

1988, At Rest
Kodak Ectachrome 64 Film
Konica 35 mm. camera
15" x 20"

1969, Spectators
Kodak Ectachrome 64 Film
Konica 35 mm. camera
15" x 20"

1987, Rear of Van - Kutztown Folk Festival
Kodak Ectachrome 64 Film
Konica 35 mm. camera
15" x 20"

1971, Evening Reflections
Kodak Ectachrome 64 Film
Konica 35 mm. camera
15" x 20"

1972, What Shall we do with Mother?
Kodak Ectachrome 64 Film
Konica 35 mm. camera
15″ x 20″

1979, The Lamp
Kodak Ectachrome 64 Film
Konica 35 mm. camera
15" x 20"

1975, Lonely Tree
Kodak Ectachrome 64 Film
Konica 35 mm. camera
15" x 20"

1976, Double Corncrib
Kodak Ectachrome 64 Film
Konica 35 mm. camera
15" x 20"

1975, Heidelberg Cemetery in Spring
Kodak Ectachrome 64 Film
Konica 35 mm. camera
15" x 20"

1979, Neon
Kodak Ectachrome 64 Film
Konica 35 mm. camera
15" x 20"

1973, White Wheel
Kodak Ectachrome 64 Film
Konica 35 mm. camera
15" x 20"

1972, Covered Bridge
Kodak Ectachrome 64 Film
Konica 35 mm. camera
15" x 20"

1984, Reflection of Ferris Wheel in Water
Kodak Ectachrome 64 Film
Konica 35 mm. camera
15" x 20"

Continued from page 31

them. Pennsylvania German themes are fully explored in 1947, and although one cannot call the year one of adventurous exploration, as in 1946, Hoffman produces excellent work in the 16 paintings of that year. In 1948 he pushed his work even further, reaching full development in his Pennsylvania German work and producing at least one masterpiece in *Symbols in the Night*, (40), an electrifying night scene of "barn star" comets reminiscent of Vincent Van Gogh's *Starry Night* (MOMA).

The eleven works of 1949 reveal a slowing of output but no diminution in energy, quality or experimentation. An element of humor and playfulness emerges strongly in *Corner of a Barnyard* (51) and *Dinner Please* (54). Some powerful architectural work is depicted in *After the Storm* (45) and *Barn Abstraction* (46). Experimentation with pattern and contrast succeeds in *Refreshers* (48) and *Sand Drifts* (49). And perhaps most surprising of all his works of this year are the symbolic portraits of four close acquaintances or relatives in *Portrait of a School Teacher* (50), *A Designer* (52), *My Aunt* (53) and *A Musician* (55).

This development and experimentation on many levels culminated in 1950 with the highest volume to date (20 paintings), some of his finest individual works (68, 71) and one of his best years ever in terms of overall liveliness and quality. Another distinctive feature of his work in 1950 is the execution of numerous pairs and series. The reworking of the same subject matter, and the extension of one work into a series, were characteristics of the modernists, as for example in Picasso's harlequin or musician series, or Stuart Davis' Eggbeater Series. Hoffman produced a series of five floral pictures in 1950 and January 1951 (61, 65, 66, 69, 76). He did an industrial series

49. Sand Drifts   **June 1949**

The Modernists were particularly fond of vacationing at artist colonies in Maine, Cape Cod, New Hope and elsewhere. Hoffman did not generally visit these colonies but did draw inspiration for his few seaside pictures from Rockport, Maine and in this case Long Beach Island. One of his finest seaside water colors is this Precisionist pattern picture of snow fences and sand drifts in sharp contrast.

50. Portrait of a School Teacher   July 1949
*This painting honors Lillian Schlegel Walter,
an elementary school teacher in Fleetwood,
Pennsylvania. She was devoted to her school,
church and husband, an excellent cook, and an
outstanding photographer and craftsperson.*

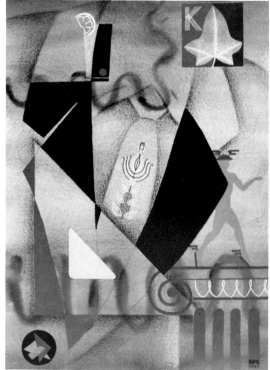

52. Portrait of a Designer   August 1949
*One of Hoffman's four symbolic portraits, this
picture represents Kenneth Bogert, a life-long
friend. Bogert attended high school with Hoffman and overlapped with him briefly at
Parsons. Bogert, another protege of Anna
Schadt, became an interior designer in Allentown. The central focus of the portrait is Bogert's
suit jacket and tie. Bogert's personal interests
are reflected in various symbols such as the
architectural column in the lower right corner.*

under Lehigh Art Alliance auspices on the Pennsylvania Power and Light power plant in Sunbury, Pennsylvania (72, 73, 74). He also continued to produce contrasting pairs of work approaching the same subject from realist and abstract perspectives.

Through this fertile, formative period from 1946-1950 Hoffman departed dramatically from his old painting style, but the revolution in his art may not have been quite as radical as it appears. The medium remained the same—water color. The subject universe expanded considerably, but Hoffman's overall body of work is still predominantly landscape, buildings and still life, as before 1946. And once he settled into a comfortable mode, Hoffman's experimentation lay within secure boundaries beyond which he rarely wandered from 1946 until giving up water color painting for color photography.

These boundaries, which were self-imposed, allowed Hoffman the degree of security which he obviously needed in order to express himself freely through color, design and theme. The chief boundaries were (1) the medium of water color, (2) a uniform size textured paper, (3) similar frames and, (4) a standard technique.

The medium of water color was the one in which Hoffman had been trained at Parsons, where he studied under Felicie

53. Portrait of my Aunt   September 1949
The third of the symbolic portrait series of 1949 is this picture of Linda Kohler Frankenfield, the aunt who lived in Kutztown, Pennsylvania. Her German heritage, Reformed faith, love of antiques and fascination for lamps are all depicted.

Howell. After only one representational painting in oil, Hoffman returned to water color and had no desire to experiment beyond that medium. The size of his paintings varied widely before 1946, but afterward Hoffman generally worked with a standard 21″ x 29″ size, with variation principally in whether the treatment was horizontal or vertical. The few exceptions are mostly slightly larger works rather than smaller ones. *Framing* seems not to have been an important consideration. Approximately 85% of the 189 works between 1946-1965 were framed, in nearly every case in a 3″ projecting frame. A small body of work remained unframed because Hoffman at the time did not regard them as worthy of framing. An example of this unframed body of work is illustrated in *Pennsylvania Dutch Summer House* (126).

Last, but vitally important in the list of boundaries for his art, was the *standard technique* or process Hoffman followed with the vast majority of his output. Normally he would have an idea at work, or see a building or scene, which he quickly transferred into a working sketch, often at the end of a long work day. Occasionally, as with

54. Dinner, Please   *November 1949*
Both the top down perspective of this painting, and the sense of humor expressed in the traditional meal of pork chop, succotash, baked potato and roll, remind one of Stuart Davis. In this case the scene probably represents Hoffman's frequent practice and love of "eating out," but it is a clever exercise in design as well.

Refreshers (48) and *Pigeon Holes* (57, 58), he would paint from a photograph. The transfer of idea to sketch usually occurred rapidly and with little reworking, for Hoffman's visual acuity enabled him to grasp the essence of design and composition easily. Then, at his leisure in the studio he had created on the third floor of his parents' home at 1345 Turner Street, Hoffman transferred and refined the sketch onto a heavy French textured paper. The studio was in a room next to his bedroom, so Hoffman could easily set his own schedule and pace. At this stage he would begin experimenting with colors and shapes, sometimes using construction paper cutouts to test colors, shapes and overall composition. When ready for final treatment, Hoffman applied his water colors. When the water

57. Pigeon Holes   January 1950
This Precisionist architectural painting is, like Refreshers, no. 48, based on a Hoffman photograph of a building at Colonial Williamsburg.

55. Portrait of a Musician   November 1949
This fourth and last symbolic portrait of 1949 is Miriam Leeds, a former violin teacher who loved cats and tea parties even though she did not believe in drinking tea herself. The choice of a musical instrument as a symbolic portrait is epitomized in Pablo Picasso's early work, for instance, Guitar (1912) in the Museum of Modern Art, New York.

color had dried thoroughly, he rubbed the work's surface with crayon, bringing out the texture of the paper beneath the water color. This technique was discovered accidentally soon after 1946, so most of his Modernist works exhibit this distinctive treatment.

Although these boundaries may seem narrow to a modern observer, and perhaps limiting to an artist's creativity, they seemed essential then to Hoffman's disciplined personality and his richly imaginative world of the mind which needed outlets for expression. He achieved freedom of expression by focusing on the process of creating art as he defined it, and voluntarily limiting his universe.

Modernism

Hoffman's definition of art is distinctly Modernist, but by the time he began painting in his new style in 1946, his interpretation of Modernism was old-fashioned, even though it had some contemporary overlays in the subject matter and color. Since he developed his distinctive style in 1946 in response to a particular life crisis, he had never previously been able to express his 1929-1932 training and exposure to

58. Pigeon Holes Abstract   **February 1950**
A companion piece to no. 57, this painting illustrates how Hoffman could treat the same subject matter in two different ways within his Modernist perspective without retreating to the pre-1946 representational style which he found so confining.

Modernism. The fact that his "new" style was already "dated" in 1946 was of no concern to Hoffman or anyone else, and in strict Modernist terms, was irrelevant. The definition of art was the artist's prerogative.

When asked if there were artists and teachers who were especially critical to the development of his work, Hoffman at first cited local teachers and friends. These included Anna Schadt, his high school art teacher; Betty Davis, in whose studio he worked for several years; William Swallow, art teacher, sculptor and friend; Verna Ruth, an English teacher at Central Junior High School, to whom Hoffman turned for assistance with color and composition issues; and Edgar Clewell, a photographer who processed Hoffman's black and white photography.

Upon further contemplation, Hoffman enlarged his world of inspiration to MOMA as an institution and Modernist artists such as Pablo Picasso and Stuart Davis. However, the fact is that Hoffman saw countless Modernist exhibits and examined numerous catalogs. His work is not patterned after any one Modernist painter but rather is synthetic and expressive of several major trends within Modernism.

Perhaps without fully realizing it at the time, Hoffman had finally in 1946 fulfilled the potential of the Modernist aesthetic to which he had been exposed from 1929-1932 in New York. Modernism was a revolt in artistic expression in Western Europe led by Paul Cezanne, Pablo Picasso and others. In their view, art was improperly dominated by the twin obsessions of skillful execution and subject matter. In traditional Western art the source of the aesthetic experience lay in nature and subject. The artist reflected, reported or realistically reproduced what was seen in nature.

In contrast, Modernism sought to restore balance to aesthetic expression by transferring the source of beauty in art to the artist, whose job it was to create art. Subject matter was transformed into symbols rather than replicas, designs rather than imitations.[3] Modernism shocked many people out of their complacency about art and provided release from centuries-old conventions for many artists.

---

60. Quilt Patterns　　　　　　　**March 1950**
Once again Hoffman was able to exercise his hallmark technique of combining traditional Pennsylvania German subjects and motifs with his flair for Modernist design.

61. Spring Blood   **March 1950**
*One of a series of wildflower pictures from
1950, this is one of the best compositions among
the small number of Hoffman's flower paintings.
It offers an interesting contrast to Andrew
Wyeth's* Quaker Ladies, *a floral which represents
the best of contemporary representational work.*

Hoffman's embrace of Modernism was in part facilitated by his lack of art historical training and his openness to new ideas concerning the sources for and nature of aesthetic expression. The emphasis of his artistic training was on drawing and design. Exposure to art history came almost entirely through museums, especially the Metropolitan Museum of Art. Although introduced to design traditions and finished artwork from Asia, the Near East and Europe, the emphasis of his Parsons training lay in inculcating certain principles of design, particularly as expressed in the art of Egypt and Greece. Museum objects provided models for drawing and sources of design and color inspiration.

Parsons in 1929-1932 was teaching the design theory of Dynamic Symmetry, the rediscovery of ancient design principles as interpreted by Jay Hambridge.[4] In contrast to static *bilateral* symmetry, where there is a central focal point flanked by mirror images, *dynamic* symmetry was art within geometry. For example, a rectangle could be "cut" or divided by diagonal and reciprocal lines to create internal movement "with control," or "expanded" by the extension of diagonal lines. Using Hambridge's system, a static rectangle could be transformed into a powerful, flowing design with internal and external dynamism.

63. Shore Lines   **April 1950**
Hoffman occasionally summered with Bethlehem artist Jerry Quier and her sisters, Vivian and Rachel, all of whom lived together in Bethlehem. Even though crippled by polio in her youth, Jerry Quier lived an active life as an artist and art teacher. This stylized fractured seascape, with both Cubist and Precisionist characteristics, is of Rockport, Massachusetts, their favorite vacation spot.

68. Williamsburg Enclosures   July 1950
One of Hoffman's most ingenious and
successful exercises in pattern making shows
Williamsburg patterns in architecture, fencing
and gardens as well as wood, brick and plants.

70. Grandmother's Kitchen   August 1950
Hoffman's maternal grandparents, the Wotrings, lived down the street at 1357 Turner Street, Allentown. In Pennsylvania German culture, grandmother's kitchen is one of the most revered spots in memory and actuality. This memory picture depicts the pattern of the linoleum on the floor as well as favored containers for cookies and milk. A favorite rooster serves as the picture's focal point.

In addition to lectures on dynamic symmetry, as mentioned above, with elaborate geometric drawing by Hoffman, the Parsons class notes outline lectures on interior design and decoration as well as perspective, among other topics. The notes on perspective comprise extensive drawings by Hoffman, for example, on different ways to draw a house. For an example of Hoffman's skill in this area one can look at *Sand Drifts* (49), a sophisticated composition of pattern and perspective.

Color theory was another specialty at Parsons. Hoffman's class notebooks from 1929-1932 contain more information and emphasis on color than any other single topic. Instruction in color theory was based on notes prepared by John M. Goodwin of Washington, D.C., which are entitled "Kindergarten of Color." Goodwin divides colors into primary (those which cannot be made by mixing other colors—red, yellow, blue); secondary (those made by mixing two primary colors—purple, green, orange); tertiary (those made by mixing two secondary colors—russet, olive, citrine); and quarternary colors (those made by mixing two tertiary colors—plum, tan, sage).

According to Goodwin, the goals of color mixing in a painting or design were harmony and complementarity. Assuming that colors were not equal in potency, the artist needed to learn to use them in different volume (space) and/or value (degree of purity and strength). The secret of color was in knowing which colors to use together, in what proportions to each other and in what intensity. To shade a color the artist would add black, to tint a color white was added. As an aid to color selection, Hoffman prepared pages of water color chips, some showing "triads" of color in proper proportion and others "quads" of color.

In the use of color in his own work after 1946, Hoffman followed the Parsons formulas more than those established by leading modernist artists such as Picasso and Stuart Davis. Davis, in particular, is far more experimental in his use of color than Hoffman, a tendency which Hoffman admired but could not replicate.[5] Nevertheless, Hoffman falls in the Modernist camp in the relative importance of color in his work, as well as in other chief areas of Modernist concern, namely composition, texture, rhythm, contrast and the exploration of themes.

Composition is essentially the organization of space. As Hoffman talks about modern art, for example Picasso, he describes Picasso's work as "filling the

74. Control House-   *October 1950*
    Sunbury Power Plant
Left to his own devices, Hoffman may never have gravitated to industrial themes. Under the auspices of a Lehigh Art Alliance program, Hoffman in the 1950s regularly painted local industries targeted by the Art Alliance. This industrial control panel at a regional Pennsylvania Power and Light plant offered a creative design opportunity.

75. The Yellow Chair   **November 1950**
Choosing the most available of subjects, namely
his own bedroom on the third floor of the family
home on Turner Street, Hoffman renders his
furniture in a direct, appealing Modernist
style reminiscent of Edward Hopper.

78. My Church, Trinity   **March 1951**

*The Art Alliance in 1951 visited local churches,
listening to talks by ministers on the symbolism
of various religious traditions. Sketching on the
spot, as they did on their visits to industries,
the artists then completed paintings in their
studios and presented them for public exhibition.
Hoffman chose his own Trinity UCC Church in
Allentown, featuring a pearwood carving of
Christ from Oberammergau, Germany. The
painting was subsequently presented to the
Good Shepherd Home in Allentown.*

space nicely," by which he means the canvas
or paper is not too crowded. Since the
Modernists were not realistically depicting
an actual scene, they did not follow a pre-
scribed way to fill the paper as would be the
case if one replicated what the eye actually
perceived. The artist is liberated from the
tyranny of reality. Hoffman and other
modernists could fill space as they chose.

Texture was another consideration in the
creation of a Modernist work. Some
artists achieved texture through use of heavy
layers of oil paint. The Cubists Georges
Braque and Pablo Picasso introduced
collage—the incorporation of elements of
paper, cloth, wood and metal into the
composition, as in Picasso's *Card Player*
(1913-1914). Hoffman experimented with
collage, but his preferred techniques for
achieving texture were (1) crayon rubbing
to bring out the texture of the heavy paper
and (2) incorporating water color patterns,
preferably plaids, into his work.

As mentioned previously, Hoffman's
work is not specifically derivative of any
one or few Modernist painters. In almost
any given painting by Hoffman one can
recognize references to specific artists, but
there is no indication that these references
are direct quotations. After 1946, Hoffman
embraced Modernist principles and fully
integrated them into his own work. His
work flourishes because he has achieved a
distinctive Modernist style. Nevertheless,
several major trends within Modernism,
namely Cubism and Precisionism, are critical
to an assessment of Hoffman's art work,
as are important individual artists, most
notably Stuart Davis.

82. Butter Molds   **May 1951**

Carved wooden butter molds were used in the eighteenth and nineteenth centuries to stamp butter slated for sale in town markets. They represent a rich and varied design tradition among the Pennsylvania Germans. Hoffman and his friend Bill Swallow collected butter molds. Here the molds provide the inspiration for a creative pattern picture reminiscent of the work of the Dutch modernist, Piet Mondrian.

Cubism is, first of all, artistic expression in abstract rather than representational (realistic) terms. The goal is to abstract or extract the essence of a subject rather than present a surface replication of a person, object or scene. Such abstraction is founded on the premise that significance increases as one moves from fact to spirit, from explicit language to symbolic language, from realism to abstraction.[6]

Coupled with the idea that the source of beauty and creativity is in the artist, rather than the subject, abstraction thus frees an artist from convention, tradition and the tyranny of "the obvious." Abstraction is "a release into profundity, symbolism and design."[7] Great art can be a picture of anything (ordinary people, the artist's studio, an eggbeater) done by a great artist, whereas prior to the Modernist movement as inaugurated by Cezanne, great art was most likely to be religious art, royal art or the art of nature. Such oversimplification is hazardous, for Dutch artists in the seventeenth century formulated an art of the everyday life, but the predominance of subject over artist was still the rule prior to the late nineteenth century.

With the principle of abstraction accepted, Modernist artists experimented in many

directions. One of the most fruitful schools of Modernism in the early twentieth century was the Cubism of Georges Braque and Pablo Picasso. Although Braque is generally credited with being the first artist to exhibit a Cubist work, Picasso and he were both developing the movement in 1907-1908. Prior to 1907 Picasso's work is still recognizably representational even though he had already moved far beyond his first realistic work in 1895-1896 of a young girl's first communion. During his long and productive lifetime Picasso developed at least two major types of Cubist expression: analytical and synthetic Cubism.

 Left:

86. The Electrical Milker   **January 1952**
Another of Hoffman's Art Alliance series, this close-up Precisionist painting of a cow's udder and an automatic milker offer all the surprise and freshness of the best of Modernist work such as Stuart Davis' Eggbeater series. Ordinary facets of life are magnified physically and symbolically, and in the process are elevated and dignified.

Right:

88. Gabriel and His Horn   **March 1952**
Religion is central to Pennsylvania German belief and practice. Hoffman's work is rarely overtly religious. Although Gabriel is mentioned in the Scriptures as the angel who will trumpet the resurrection of the Christian dead from all ages, here Hoffman is playfully rendering an existing tin weathervane and setting it in the night sky lit by a full moon.

In analytical Cubism one divides or dissects a surface in order to analyze it. The subject — a person, still life, landscape — is broken apart and reordered, often in abstract shapes so that the subject is barely, if at all, recognizable. In Picasso's work these pictures were often largely monochromatic, with subtle shadings of color and tone. The sharp lines and edges also tended to dissolve as Picasso moved to the edges of the painting, similar to the fading of background and distant fuzziness of objects in a close-up photograph.[8]

In synthetic Cubism the emphasis is not on division and analysis of parts but rather on the reconstituted whole. Fragments are recombined, although not always in their realistic or logical order, into larger and often more recognizable patterns and shapes. The decorative qualities of painting are vital to synthetic Cubism, so color and texture characterize these works. The colors are often quite bright and the paintings are at times of mixed media.[9] Collage was an invention of the Cubists, with Braque probably the pioneer. They used it very effectively in portraits, where bits and pieces of paper, textile, wood and metal could relate to the subject at hand, often in witty and symbolic ways.[10]

From 1913, the date of the New York Armory Show where Picasso displayed

96. Red Chimney   **February 1953**
Precisionists such as Sheeler and Charles Demuth followed the early twentieth century "Ash Can School" in using urban streets, alleys and rooftops for the first time as artistic subject matter. In this case Hoffman portrays the view from his Turner Street studio window.

98. Neighborhood Nocturne   April 1953
Using one of his photographs to concentrate on a rooftop view, Hoffman sees primarily a contrasting pattern of roof angles and window rectangles. Although his geometric patterning predominates, Hoffman is also symbolizing the human dimension of a neighborhood community, where each house has eyes if not ears.

103. Pennsylvania Dutch 103   December 1953
During the 1950s public interest in Pennsylvania Dutch culture flourished. The embarrassments of German aggression during World War II lay comfortably behind. Appreciation of American culture was seen as a necessary antidote to the threat of communism. In the cultural climate of the 1950s, Pennsylvania Germans like Hoffman could proudly promote their cultural heritage. Many of Hoffman's finest Pennsylvania Dutch paintings date from this era of cultural self-consciousness, which also saw the founding of magazines and folk festivals dedicated to the understanding and perpetuation of Pennsylvania German culture.

eight works and the American public saw the vitality and significance of Modernism for the first time, an artist had choices available to him or her that the world had not previously known. Picasso claimed he painted subjects "as I think them," not "as I see them"[11] and he also relied on "personal experience and the given of his immediate environment as the point of departure for his art."[12] Even though considered outrageous by some, Picasso could paint his mistresses, his friends or his studio rather than the traditional canon of wealthy patrons, political leaders and natural scenes. Picasso also opened the artist's world in another way. From 1915 on he pursued several variations or styles of painting simultaneously, a radical departure in artistic practice for his time.[13]

Some of Hoffman's works are clearly Cubist, for example, his four symbolic portraits. Like the Cubists, Hoffman does not render a physical likeness of his subjects. They are not sitters in any conventional sense. The portraits are an abstract collage of symbols and references to personal attributes. Consequently, the finished portrait delves beneath the surface of likeness to represent inner qualities of character and personality. There are many Modernist precedents for such abstract portraits, for example, Francis Picabia's famous "spark-plug" *Portrait of an American Girl* (1915), Arthur Dove's *Portrait of Ralph Dusenberry*

104. Lower Town   **January 1954**
This Precisionist urban landscape is also a result of Hoffman's 1953 trip to Quebec. The focal point of the painting is a Pepsi Cola billboard.

(1924), Marsden Hartley's *One Portrait of One Woman* (1916) and *Portrait of a German Officer* (1913), and Picasso's own *Student With a Pipe* (1913-1914). Even though Cubism, as one of the major forces in Modernism, helped set the tone for Hoffman's work and clearly shaped his approach in specific works, one would not characterize Hoffman primarily as a Cubist. The corpus of his work (189 pictures) reveals that Hoffman's identity lies more clearly within another major branch of Modernism, namely Precisionism.

Precisionism

The Precisionists, like the Cubists, also practiced abstraction, but they emphasized pure geometric abstraction and simplification

106. Portrait of Allentown April 1954
An abstract and sympathetic portrait of Hoffman's hometown.

108. Pennsylvania   *September 1954*
      Dutch Farm

An entire farm, including a pair of ducks on water, is abstracted into geometry and pattern and then recombined in this ambitious work of synthetic Cubism. The result, however, is more reminiscent of Edward Hopper than Pablo Picasso.

of form. Consequently, the Precisionists could retain much Realism in their work. Artists Charles Sheeler, Charles Demuth, Morton Schamberg and Ralston Crawford best represent early twentieth-century Precisionism. All of the leading Precisionists had strong Philadelphia and southeastern Pennsylvania connections, often by birth as well as training.

Charles Demuth (1883-1935) was the only son of a prominent Lancaster, Pennsylvania German family. The Demuths for many generations had operated a tobacco shop in downtown Lancaster. Demuth, crippled by illness at age four and always lame and frail, spent two years at the local Franklin and Marshall Academy before undertaking formal art training at the Pennsylvania Academy of Fine Arts in Philadelphia and in Paris. Although always retaining his residence in Lancaster, Demuth also lived in New York and various artist colonies. From the time of his first exhibit in New York in 1914, Demuth moved in the highest modernist circles.[14]

Demuth's work expresses the geometry of the Cubists although with the use of more pure and precise geometric forms. The chief subject matter of his work is urban architecture and industrial design. Always a strong regionalist, Demuth reflects his Lancaster heritage in his work. Most of the buildings he painted were within easy

---

109. Pennsylvania Brick   *October 1954*
    End Barns

Brick barns were less common in Pennsylvania German culture regions than log or stone ones. They appealed to Hoffman as an architectural type because their air vents offered an opportunity for creative patterning by masons of long ago. Once again Hoffman superimposes layers of patterning in an intricacy reflective of Mondrian.

walking distance of his Lancaster home, or were visible from the train he rode regularly from Lancaster to Philadelphia.[15] His architectural works best reflect his Precisionist style. They are marked by geometric hard edges, often done in oil. However, Demuth's range was part of his greatness. Many of his finest works are delicate water colors, often floral compositions. Demuth never confined his creativity to one style or subject matter.[16]

The significance of Precisionists like Demuth lies in the fact that they offered the American public a relatively benign transition into Modernism. Fully blown, avant garde European Modernism, as expressed by Picasso, Matisse, Braque, Klee and others, was a radical aesthetic movement. The shift from representational art was a shocking and difficult step for Americans in general and even American

artists. Many American artists dabbled in the more extreme forms of Modernism but few internalized its spirit in their work. The Precisionists emerged in the 1920s as a unique blend of Modernism's abstract principles and American Realism. Choosing the American industrial and urban landscapes as themes, the Precisionists offered Americans a vernacular version of Modernism.[17]

Charles Sheeler was probably the Precisionist par excellence and the one closest in spirit to Hoffman. Although the bulk of his work represents urban forms and industrial technology and reflects Sheeler's enthusiasm for man-made things, Sheeler is one of the few American modernists, along with Georgia O'Keefe, to explore rural subjects such as barns and Shaker buildings.[18] From his Barn Abstraction in

110. In a Pennsylvania   **January 1955**
      Dutch Kitchen
The kitchen, its implements and most of all its delectable products are a recurrent theme for Hoffman. In this case we see trivets, cookie cutters, coffeepot, sugar bowl and measuring spoon, among other items, symbolizing the process of baking as well as the moment of final enjoyment of the end products.

116. Pennsylvania Wrought Iron   July 1955
*Hoffman brings inanimate objects to life
through a series of design abstractions, much
as the blacksmith initially wrought red hot iron
into functional items with decorative flair.*

117. Pennsylvania Dutch   September 1955
      Brick End Barns

*A companion work for no. 109, which can be
seen as a detail or compressed abstraction of
this overall composition. Barns were the most
popular subject matter for Hoffman, which gives
his precisionism even more of a rural slant than
Charles Sheeler, whose work is predominantly
urban/industrial, with some important
paintings devoted to barns specifically
or rural subjects generally.*

1917 to historic architecture based on his
sojourn to Williamsburg, Virginia in 1935,
Sheeler throughout his career turned to rural
and historical motifs.[19] He is distinctive in
that, unlike Demuth, he stayed within the
Precisionist framework for over thirty
years, becoming its foremost proponent.
Sheeler is, therefore, the Precisionist to
whom Hoffman is most closely related in
subject matter and technique. They also
have a bond in their common enthusiasm
for art photography.

As early as 1914 Sheeler experimented
with art photography in the Doylestown
Studio which he shared with Milton
Schamberg. Through photography he
explored compositions, details and scenes
which he would later copy in his paintings.[20] By 1919, after Schamberg's death,
Sheeler had moved to New York, where he
photographed New York architecture and
began painting his first Precisionist urban
paintings. Over a thirty-year period he
refined and elaborated his style of work
which ranged from semi-abstract to
photo-realism. In some cases he used photographs to provide reference materials for
his pictures.[21]

Modernist painting and art photography
developed in tandem in the early twentieth
century. The individual in America most
supportive of Modernist artwork before
World War I was photographer Alfred
Stieglitz, whose 291 Studio gallery promoted
art photography and Modernist painting.
Although most Modernists were not photo-
graphers, a few, like Sheeler, used it to
great advantage.

Sheeler was an accomplished photographer by 1917, when his Precisionist
style began to mature. In fact, his Precisionism probably owes a great deal to his
skill and experience as a photographer and
may be why the "hard edge" geometry of

Precisionism appealed to him more than geometric abstraction. At first he had taken up commercial photography to support his painting. In time, however, he experimented with the camera to explore form, light and texture, and photographed starkly modern pictures of barns and stairwells. In doing so, Sheeler began "to explore compositions in which abstract form was achieved through a Cubist cropping and flattening of pictorial elements. . . ."[22] In similar fashion, Hoffman explored photography as an artistic medium upon his return to Allentown. By 1939 he was accomplished enough to enter a black and white photograph in competition at the New York World's Fair, in which he won first prize. Photography remains a medium of expression for Hoffman to this day. As long as he was still painting, photography was both an adjunct to painting

---

122. Spring in Pennsylvania   April 1956
The title of this painting does not have an obvious connection to the flat, one dimensional bank barn presented in this patterned rendition of Hoffman's favorite theme.

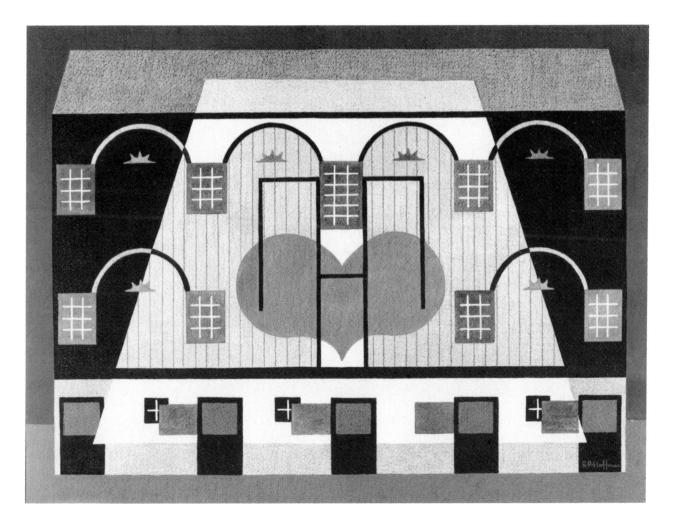

123. Lighthouse   **May 1956**

*Hoffman over time executed a series of
exceptionally fine Precisionist works on
architecture. In subject matter and treatment
they are frequently departures from his norm.
This Hopper-like painting is of a lighthouse
complex in Rockport, Massachusetts.*

and an independent form of artistic expression. In 1965 Hoffman put aside his brushes for good, but not his camera. As he ceased painting, he shifted from black and white photography to color photography and launched himself into a new era of creative expression.

Stuart Davis

Before concluding that Richard Peter Hoffman's Modernist paintings fall most logically within a Precisionist framework, it is necessary to look at the work of another American Modernist whose work Hoffman knew and openly admired in 1946. Stuart Davis was probably America's best-known Modernist, justly recognized for his murals at Radio City Music Hall, his paintings and his outspoken art theories.

Few painters are equally skillful at creating art and articulating theory. Davis, however, was a philosopher as well as an artist.

> Art is not the pursuit of some ideal canon of beauty...but a struggle to realize spiritual values innate in (the artist) in relation to the world.... Art's purpose is ...to create forms that embody the psychological content of (the artist's) perceptions and emotions in response to that subject matter.[23]

For Davis, as well as other Modernist artists, replication or representational art is unsatisfactory because it does not express the psychological reality and creativity of the artist. Consequently, the Modernist artist wants to create art which "expresses the psychological temper of some aspect of the society...and of his own temperament in relation to that society."[24]

> His purpose is never to counterfeit a subject but to develop a new subject. His purpose is also to live in giving importance to certain qualities in himself, which everyone presumably possesses, but which relatively few cultivate.[25]

Stuart Davis studied art under Robert Henri in New York from 1910-1913, where he learned how to draw and where he discovered the "raw vitality" of contemporary urban life. He was one of the many American artists shocked and exhilarated by the 1913 Armory Show, which he later called the "single greatest influence" on his work because it taught him how to think of color objectively and to see paintings as their own reality rather than replicas of reality.[26] For example, instead of thinking of all trees as green-leaved and of an

129. Sticks and Stones   *November 1956*
The range and quality of Hoffman's work in 1956 is matched only by his 1940s paintings. Sticks and Stones represents yet another departure for him as he creates a still life of distinction which hints at the work of masters such as Jean Miro.

identifiable shape, Davis could now paint a green tree red and create a new language of forms, in which his trees, if he so chose, might not look like conventional trees in nature.[27]

Davis displayed five of his own works at the Armory Show, but he was not familiar with modern art as exhibited there by European avant garde artists. Davis especially appreciated the introduction to Matisse, Gauguin and Van Gogh because of their "broad stylization of form" and "non-imitative use of color" and for "an objective order" which he saw in their work and felt was missing from his own. He resolved to become a Modernist artist.[28]

Introduced to Alfred Stieglitz through the Armory Show, Davis began to meet other Modernist artists in the Stieglitz circle, including Charles Demuth. To 1920 Davis' work is experimental, showing influences of Van Gogh, Cezanne, Picasso, Braque and others. For a time he embraced synthetic Cubism. But Davis during the 1920s was also experimenting with color and geometry and developing a distinctive style which stressed the formal qualities of design and decoration over subject matter. In this development he incorporated Jay Hambidge's doctrine of Dynamic Symmetry, the same system of geometric relationships governing shapes and ratios of solid to void that was taught to Hoffman at Parsons in the early 1930s.[29]

With the start of his Eggbeater series in 1927-1928, where for a year Davis painted variations on an eggbeater nailed to a table in his New York studio, Davis established his unique Modernist style, with its distinctive emphasis on color, and in effect caught up with the European masters of Modernism. In this context, his extended trip to Paris in 1928-1929 was anti-climactic. Unlike many other Americans, for whom Paris was critical to the development or refor-mulation of their work, Davis was already working out his theories by himself.

Nevertheless, the absence from New York had its effect. As with Hoffman, Davis arrived back in New York late in 1929. The size and vitality of the city struck him with new force, particularly the recently completed Chrysler building. The stock market crash also brought home the vulnerability of urban, industrial society.[30] From 1929-1932 Davis focused intensely on New York as he further refined his geometric and colorful style. In 1931-1932 most of his designs were built out of angular and rectangular shapes which he executed in black and white. Then in 1933 he began reintroducing color. His work in the early '30s, although within a Cubist framework, is a distinct synthesis of design, color and subject matter (New York) which Davis called "Color-Space Compositions" or "Events". At one point Davis commented that the artist's role was to be a "cool spectator reporter at an arena of hot events." Even though his work concentrated on design and color, Davis did not intend to be politically neutral or lacking in social conscience.[31]

Ever since his pre-World War I experience creating cartoons for *The Masses*, an influential leftist magazine published in New York, Davis supported leftist politics. In the mid 1930s Davis espoused Marxism but never accepted communist party efforts to force artists to adhere to orthodox Marxist art theory. In the late 1930s he endeavored to walk a line between Marxist social realism, American regionalist realism (which he saw as politically right wing and devoid of social conscience), and geometric abstraction.

The latter, which emphasized pure form as in the work of Piet Mondrian, was to him meaningless to anyone but an arcane artistic priesthood. Davis' goal, on the other

133. Schnipples   **April 1957**
Schnipples is a Pennsylvania German dialect term for odds and ends, paper cuttings and what is left in the pan. In this case the cut outs are generally identifiable and so are not technically wasted odds and ends. They are actually paper patterns of the type the artist could manipulate to test design ideas, a technique used frequently in this geometric work.

hand, was to balance the formal aspects of painting (design, form, color) with meaningful social content, and to express himself in socially relevant abstract art.[32] During most of this period, from 1933-1939, it should be noted that Davis was employed on a New Deal WPA project, painting murals for New York's new Radio City Music Hall.

Clearly, from 1950, Hoffman was following an artistic progression similar to what Stuart Davis had experienced from 1913-1932. Davis described his growth to artistic maturity in three stages.[33] First, he needed to assert the artist's right of control over subject matter, to break the tyranny of replication. Davis' revelation on this matter came at the Armory Show in 1913. He did not feel the triumph until the Eggbeater series of 1927-1928 where, by painting the same mundane object from different perspectives, he liberated himself. For Hoffman the experience was more conversion-like, occurring in May 1946.

The second stage for Davis was to control color by recognizing that the perceived color of any subject could change over time according to the artist's memory or will. Davis was an avid student of the color theories of his era and systematically experimented with color systems, for example, that of H.G. Maratta. Hoffman after 1946 basically applied to his work the new color system

138. Seaport USA   **July 1957**
Rockport, Massachusetts inspires a rare marine abstract, complete with a lobster, presumably imported from Maine.

he had learned at Parsons. Consequently, his colors are not as vibrant and original as Davis' but tend to reflect more the palette acceptable to the commercial design world of the 1930s, '40s and '50s.

The third stage for Davis was control over the relationships of shapes, solids and voids in the design of his paintings.

> Using the same still-life as subject (e.g., the eggbeater) I mentally simplified the objects and the space perspective into arbitrary geometric shapes and arbitrarily moved them about in the several compositions to suit my emotional preference. I thereby established my authority over the shape and space of the subject and introduced Time into Form....[34]

Hoffman similarly manipulated shapes in his designs, often by the use of paper cutouts from colored construction paper and followed, to some degree, the Hambright system of Dynamic Symmetry which he internalized in his years of rigorous training at Parsons.

As one compares the actual works of Stuart Davis and Richard Peter Hoffman, one would be hard put to find any direct link between them. The affinity, however, lies in the degree to which both of these American Modernists were exposed to and internalized the prevailing modern art theory of the 1920s. Both established their styles

140. Moravian College   *August 1957*
A composite Precisionist institutional portrait of Moravian College in Bethlehem, Pennsylvania.

according to 1920s principles, even though Hoffman does not overtly express his style until 1946, by which time Davis had continued to progress to a position as dean of American modern art in New York. In 1945 Davis' achievements were recognized in a retrospective exhibition at the Museum of Modern Art.

HOFFMAN, 1950-1965

Painting represented a major force in Richard Peter Hoffman's life from 1946, but it was not his only or even his primary interest in terms of time commitment. Hoffman never devoted full time to painting, nor painted to support himself financially. Hoffman's spare time was also filled with activities other than painting. A remarkably detailed set of diaries kept by Hoffman from 1935 to the present reveals Richard Peter's industrious, even daunting, schedule of social activity through the years. The diaries indicate that Hoffman was, and is, an indefatigable traveler, a prodigious theater-goer and an active participant in the civic and cultural life of Allentown. The extensive time commitments for his rich and varied diet of activity seemed to allow little time for his painting. Hoffman's secret lay in the dis-

142. From the Orient   November 1957
Once again, objects in his own suite of modern furnishings allow Hoffman to capture the design essence of relatively mundane and inexpensive things. This abstract skillfully combines the forms of a Japanese lantern, a table, a potted plant and a seashell to achieve a free flowing design of exceptional movement.

ciplined pattern of his life as a single man and the careful balance which he maintained among his many interests.

Except for May 1946, an intense period of artistic discovery and liberation depicted below, Hoffman's records show that he never painted more than three paintings in one month, and then only five times over nineteen years. The normal pattern was one to two paintings per month in active months, namely January through July, and zero to one paintings during inactive months, from August through December. The accompanying chart illustrates Hoffman's output by months and years.

144. First National Bank — February 1958
The bank, located at Seventh and Hamilton Streets in Allentown, together with its Nineteenth Street branch in Allentown and its branch in Emmaus, are portrayed in Precisionist style. Hoffman's father served on the Board of Directors. Hoffman worked as a teller at the Nineteenth Street branch after leaving the family grocery business.

ARTISTIC PRODUCTION — 20 YEARS

	1946	47	48	49	50	51	52	53	54	55	56	57	58	59	60	61	62	63	64	65	Monthly Totals
Jan.	-	2	1	1	2	1	1	1	1	1	2	2	1	0	1	1	2	0	0	1	21
Feb.	-	0	2	1	2	0	1	2	0	1	1	0	1	1	2	1	1	0	0	0	16
Mar.	-	2	2	2	3	2	2	0	0	0	1	1	1	0	1	1	1	0	0	1	20
Apr.	-	2	0	0	2	1	1	1	2	0	1	1	1	1	1	0	0	0	0	0	14
May	4	2	2	0	2	3	1	1	0	2	1	2	1	1	0	0	0	0	0	1	23
June	2	2	1	1	0	0	1	0	1	1	1	2	1	1	2	0	0	1	0	-	17
July	2	1	1	2	3	1	1	1	0	2	2	1	1	1	3	0	2	0	0	-	24
Aug.	1	1	3	1	1	0	0	0	0	0	0	1	2	1	1	1	0	0	1	-	14
Sept.	1	1	0	1	1	0	0	1	1	1	0	1	1	1	1	1	0	0	0	-	12
Oct.	2	0	1	0	3	1	0	0	1	0	1	0	1	0	0	0	0	0	1	-	11
Nov.	1	2	2	2	1	1	1	1	0	0	1	1	0	0	0	1	0	0	0	-	14
Dec.	0	1	0	0	0	0	0	1	0	0	0	0	0	0	0	0	1	0	0	-	3
Total	13	16	15	11	20	10	9	9	6	8	12	13	10	7	12	6	6	1	2	3	189

149. Illusion   **July 1958**

*One of the marks of an excellent artist is that
he never stops experimenting. Although Hoffman works within a Modernist framework, his
art develops over time, changing dramatically
in 1946 and evolving in several different ways
after 1946. However, Hoffman rarely extends
his work to the Abstract Expressionism of the
American Modernists who succeeded Stuart
Davis and Charles Sheeler, for example de
Kooning, Pollock, Motherwell, Rothko and
Frankenthaler. "Illusion" appears to be the
work of another artist, but is not. Hoffman
did not recognize Abstract Expressionism as a
new opportunity. After one other experiment
with it, he retreated to safer, less free-wheeling
design where he felt more confident of his
ability to control his artistic expression.*

The inescapable fact revealed by a study of Hoffman's painting habits is that he painted at his convenience for his own reasons, choosing to fall into a part-time routine and pattern. Although outings by the Lehigh Art Alliance and an occasional commission might dictate subject matter or number of paintings, generally Hoffman painted for himself, not an audience. Although some paintings were sold to corporations, friends, private collectors and museums, Hoffman's Precisionist work was not widely appreciated or known. Consequently, market demand did not drive Hoffman to variations in his work or to greater output.

Such an observation is not a judgment of the quality of Hoffman's painting, nor a criticism of his work. Many artists now canonized in the halls of art historical scholarship died in poverty and obscurity, unrecognized by the art critics and public of their time, so sale of works of art has never been a reliable criterion for assessing aesthetic merit. However, the fact that Hoffman's art was not market driven does lead to a final personal rather than social assessment of the significance of his work.

Modern art, for Hoffman, seems to have been a way of bringing needed order to a creative, but at times confusing inner world. Through design, which was his strong suit, Hoffman pacified the chaotic and ambivalent feelings of his young adulthood. Representational art, the skillful manipulation of materials and technique in the imitation of nature, was not enough. He needed a more creative release for the powerful emotions generated by parental authority, sexual ambivalence, self doubt and cultural anxiety. Hoffman was caught between several worlds, all of which provided some pleasure and meaning for his busy life and yet created friction as

well. Naturally, in real life one could only hope to control the intensity and multiplicity of these forces. In his art world Hoffman could reign as undisputed master. Precisionism, as a Modernist approach to art, allowed Hoffman to strike a balance between the natural world which he revered and the inner world of his mind and soul. The "hard edge" geometry of Precisionism allowed Hoffman to control relationships and spiritual strivings. Its openness in regard to subject matter allowed him to address the full range of emotions and themes he faced in his fertile inner world.

The works illustrated in this volume are generally representative of the full range of Hoffman's work from 1946-1965, with a weighting to Pennsylvania German themes and images for the purpose of this volume

158. Pennsylvania Landscape   **August 1959**
Hoffman's retreat to familiar territory produced more predictable but less exciting work, such as this Lehigh County landscape. Although reminiscent of his first landscape in May 1946, this painting thirteen years later lacks the spontaneity and promise of that pioneer work.

and to earlier works from 1946-1950 because the period looms large in the development of his artistic style. The years 1946 and 1950 are among the two most productive years of Hoffman's career as a water colorist, in volume and quality.

After 1950's banner year, Hoffman's output and quality declined dramatically in 1951. He produced ten works in 1951 as opposed to twenty in 1950, and most of his work appears to have been done under Lehigh Art Alliance auspices. Although Hoffman does produce two important series on newspaper printing and dairying, there is little sense of experimentation in these years, and many themes explored from 1946-1950 are left fallow. Even the Pennsylvania German emphasis of the early years suffers from neglect.

In 1954, the Pennsylvania German theme reemerges with vigor, perhaps spurred by the Broadway production of *Plain and Fancy*. Hoffman saw the play and credits it with having a significant impact on his own view of and interest in his Pennsylvania German heritage. The Pennsylvania German theme remains strong through 1955, then tapers off once again even though his work overall exhibits vitality and strength through 1958. In 1957 and 1958, instead of pursuing Pennsylvania German themes, Hoffman shifts noticeably to experimentation with geometric abstraction and exhibits strong interest in paintings of architecture and community. Generally speaking, the paintings executed from 1954-1958 are among the best of Hoffman's work, even though the output is less than in the crucial years 1946-1950.

From 1959-1962 Hoffman continues to emphasize geometric abstraction in his work, but loses the ability to progress with it. In 1963 he returns strongly to Pennsylvania German themes for the third time in his painting career and continues to work

on them until 1965, when he suddenly abandoned water color painting for color photography.

In retrospect, Hoffman himself has no regrets about the decision to stop painting. Personally, the reasons why he had started painting in a new style in 1946 were no longer acute concerns. Hoffman was happy and busy in 1965 and painting had lost its usefulness to him. In addition, he found that people were generally more receptive to his art photography than his painting. Hoffman laid down the brush in 1965 and never looked back.

160. Looking Upward   ***January 1960***
This Art Alliance project addresses the subject of religion and freedom in memory of Allentown's role in the American Revolutionary War. The painting now hangs in the public Liberty Bell Shrine of Allentown's Zion Church.

FOOTNOTES

1. *Allentown Morning Call*, June 10, 1932.
2. *Allentown Chronicle and News*, June 21, 1935.
3. Ralph M. Pearson. *The Modern Renaissance in American Art* (New York: Harper and Bros., 1954), 14, 17, 20.
4. Hoffman Notebook, July 11, 1932 lecture by Mrs. Franklin.
5. Interview with Richard Peter Hoffman, June 2, 1989.
6. Pearson, 197.
7. Pearson, 201.
8. William Rubin. *Picasso In The Collection of The Museum of Modern Art* (New York: The Museum of Modern Art, 1972), 62, 66.
9. Ibid., 76.
10. Ibid., 51.
11. Ibid., 51.
12. Ibid., 51.
13. Ibid., 103.
14. Karen Tsujimoto. *Images of America: Precisionist Painting and Modern Photography* (Seattle and London: University of Washington Press, 1982), 186.
15. Betsy Fahlman. *Pennsylvania Modern: Charles Demuth of Lancaster* (Philadelphia, Pennsylvania: Philadelphia Museum of Art, 1983), 17.
16. Ibid., 7.
17. Tsujimoto, 20-21.
18. Ibid., 73.
19. Ibid., 83.
20. Ibid., 75.
21. Ibid., 85.
22. Ibid., 75.
23. Pearson, 204-205.
24. Ibid., 205.
25. James J. Sweeney. *Stuart Davis* (New York: Museum of Modern Art, 1945), 55.
26. John R. Lane. *Stuart Davis Art and Theory* (New York: The Brooklyn Museum, 1978), 9, 15.
27. Sweeney, 9-10.
28. Lane, 10.
29. Ibid., 10, 14-15.
30. Bruce Weber. *Stuart Davis' New York* (West Palm Beach, Florida: Norton Gallery and School of Art, 1985), 10.
31. Lane, 27, 29-30.
32. Ibid., 35-36.
33. Ibid., 17-18.
34. Ibid., 17.

175. Bird Cage **September 1961**
Bird trees are a traditional motif in Pennsylvania German artistic and craft traditions. Birds appear on nearly all forms of folk cultural expressions. Hoffman's treatment of the subject is somewhat unusual in that his birds are nearly always in cages, in contrast to free-standing birds of Pennsylvania German folk art. In this case Hoffman has even put a carved, wooden bird tree in a cage set on a window sill and circumscribed by more boundaries.

PAINTINGS BY RICHARD PETER HOFFMAN • 1946-1965

In the following list, exhibitions in Allentown have no location designated; towns without designated states are in Pennsylvania. Ownership is given only for those pieces in public institutions. Awards at exhibitions are stated in parenthesis behind the show's place.

1. Five Pines Farm, water color, May 1946.
Civic Little Theatre, 1946; Don-Mart Interiors, Reading, 1947; Tow Path House, New Hope, 1948-1949; Good Shepherd Home, 1949; Circulating Picture Club, 1949; Art Museum, 1962; Hazleton Art League, 1966.

2. Country Forms, water color, May 1946.
Art Museum, 1946; Civic Little Theatre, 1947; Don-Mart Interiors, Reading, 1947; Aurand Shop, 1947; Harry Salpeter Gallery, New York, 1948; Tow Path House, New Hope, 1949; Circulating Picture Club, 1949; Art Museum, 1962; Hazleton Art League, 1966.

3. Beach Objects - Low Tide, water color, May 1946.
Lehigh University, 1947; Don-Mart Interiors, Reading, 1947.

4. Papa Is All, water color, May 1946.
Civic Little Theatre, 1947; Don-Mart Interiors, 1947; Aurand Shop, 1947; Lancaster Country Store, Brownstown, 1950-1951; Lehigh Art Alliance, Bethlehem, 1964-1965; Hazleton Art League, 1966.

5. Pennsylvania Dutch Designs, water color, June 1946.
Lehigh University, 1947.

6. Taufschein Bird, water color, June 1946.
Lehigh University, 1947; Civic Little Theatre, 1947; Don-Mart Interiors, Reading, 1947; Delaware Book Shop, New Hope, 1947; Aurand Shop, 1947; PA Freeman, Inc., 1948; Free Library, 1950; Folk Festival, Kutztown, 1950.

7. Beach Sunbather, water color, July 1946.
Lehigh University, 1947; Don-Mart Interiors, Reading, 1947; Aurand Shop, 1947; Harry Salpeter Gallery, New York, 1948.

8. Pennsylvania Dutch Barn, water color, July 1946.
Lehigh University, 1947; Civic Little Theatre, 1947; Don-Mart Interiors, Reading, 1947; Tow Path House, New Hope, 1947; Harry Salpeter Gallery, New York, 1949; Free Library, 1950; Folk Festival, Kutztown, 1950; Lancaster Country Store, Brownstown, 1951; Montclair (NJ) Art Museum, 1952.

9. Circus Big Top, water color, August 1946.
Lehigh University, 1946; Don-Mart Interiors, Reading, 1947; Tow Path House, New Hope, 1947; Harry Salpeter Gallery, New York, 1949; Gallery Studio, Bethlehem, 1950; Aurand Shop, 1950; Liberty High School, Bethlehem, 1951; Circulating Picture Club, 1978-1981.

10. Jack-In-The-Pulpit, crayon and water color, September 1946.
Lehigh University, 1947; Don-Mart Interiors, Reading, 1947; Aurand Shop, 1947; Harry Salpeter Gallery, New York, 1948; P.A. Freeman, Inc., 1948; Circulating Picture Club, 1948; Meierhans Gallery, Hagersville, 1959.

11. Square and Circle, tempera and crayon abstract, October 1946.

12. Falling Leaves, water color and crayon, October 1946.
Aurand Shop, 1947; Harry Salpeter Gallery, New York, 1948; Muhlenberg College, 1948; Good Shepherd Home, 1949; Circulating Picture Club, 1970.

13. Autumn Glory, tempera and crayon, November 1946.
Muhlenberg College, 1947; Aurand Shop, 1947; P. A. Freeman, Inc., 1948; Circulating Picture Club, 1948; Meierhans Gallery, Hagersville, 1959.

14. Among The Hills, tempera, January 1947.
Don-Mart Interiors, Reading, 1947; Aurand Shop, 1947; Harry Salpeter Gallery, New York, 1948; P. A. Freeman, Inc., 1948; Moravian College, 1959 (Founders' Day Art Contest, First Honorable Mention); Circulating Picture Club, 1948.

15. Distelfink and Heart, tempera, January 1947.
Civic Little Theatre, 1947; Don-Mart Interiors, Reading, 1947.

16. Alley by Night, tempera, March 1947.
Don-Mart Interiors, Reading, 1947; Aurand Shop, 1947; Philadelphia Water Color Club, Art Alliance, Philadelphia, 1948; Audubon Artists exhibition, New York, 1948; Brill's Artists' Supply Store, 1945-1955; Lehigh Art Alliance, Lehigh University, 1955; Liberty High School, Bethlehem, 1955-1956; Meierhans Gallery, Hagersville, 1959; Art Museum, 1962.

17. Pennsylvania Dutch Cookie Cutters, water color and crayon, March 1947.
Delaware River Artists Group Show, Milford, NJ, 1947; Tow Path House, New Hope, 1947; Don-Mart Interiors, Reading, 1947-1948; Harry Salpeter Gallery, New York, 1948; P. A. Freeman, Inc., 1948; Delaware Book Shop, New Hope, 1948; Bethlehem Women's Club, 1948; Distelfink Gift Shop, 1950; Free Library, 1950; Folk Festival, Kutztown, 1950; Lancaster Country Store, Brownstown, 1950; Montclair (NJ) Art Museum, 1952; Folk Festival, Kutztown, 1953; Glockenspiel, Kutztown, 1955; Little Studio, Gimbels, New York, 1955-1956; Southern Lehigh Jr.-Sr. High School, 1956-1957; Meierhans Gallery, Hagersville, 1959; Mercersburg Academy, 1959; Universalist Church, Philadelphia, 1960; Glockenspiel, Kutztown, 1961; Ruth Hager Gallery, Lancaster, 1961-1962; Woodmere Gallery, Chestnut Hill, 1963; Hazleton Art League, 1966; Lehigh Art Alliance, Bethlehem, 1974;

18. Fish and the Beach, crayon and water color, April 1947.
Philadelphia Water Color Club, Art Alliance, Philadelphia, 1948; Tow Path House, New Hope, 1948; Art Museum, 1948-1949; Phillips Mill Spring exhibition, near New Hope, 1950; Aurand Shop, 1950; Lehigh University, 1952; Parkland High School, Orefield, 1955.

19. Taufschein, Pennsylvania Dutch Birth Certificate Designs, water color and tempera, April 1947.
Don-Mart Interiors, Reading, 1947-1948; Aurand Shop, 1948; Harry Salpeter Gallery, New York, 1948-1949; Free Library, 1950; Folk Festival, Kutztown 1950; Lancaster Country Store, Brownstown, 1951; Montclair (NJ) Art Museum, 1952; Harcum Junior College, Bryn Mawr, 1952; Folk Festival, Kutztown 1952; Pennsylvania Dutch Seminar, Wernersville, 1952; Folk Festival, Selinsgrove, 1952; Woodmere Gallery, Chestnut Hill, 1952; Pace-Setter shop. 1952-1953; Folk Festival, Kutztown 1953; Art Museum, 1962.

20. Feathered Flight; Bird and The Elements, water color and tempera, May 1947
Aurand Shop, 1947; Harry Salpeter Gallery, New York, 1948; P. A. Freeman, Inc., 1948; Woodmere Gallery, Chestnut Hill, 1950; Lancaster Country Store, Brownstown, 1950-1951; Lehigh University, 1952; Moby Dick Book Shop, 1952; Cedar Crest College, 1955; Kramer's Music House, 1956-1957; Southern Lehigh School, Coopersburg, 1957-1958; Meierhans Gallery, Hagersville, 1959.

21. Skunk Cabbage, water color and crayon, May 1947

Lehigh University, 1947; Harry Salpeter Gallery, New York, 1948; P. A. Freeman, Inc., 1948; Gallery Studio, Bethlehem, 1950; Pace-Setter Shop, 1953; Meierhans Gallery, Hagersville, 1959; Moravian Seminary, Green Pond, 1970; Circulating Picture Club, 1978-1981.

22. Out by The Pennsylvania Dutch Barn; tempera, June 1947.

Tow Path House, New Hope, 1947-1948; Harry Salpeter Gallery, New York, 1948-1949; Free Library, 1950; Lancaster Country Store, Brownstown, 1950-1951; Liberty High School, Bethlehem, 1951; Folk Festival, Kutztown, 1954; Betty Seidel Gift Shops, Cherryville, 1955; Glockenspiel, Kutztown, 1955-1959.

23. Chicken on The Farm, water color and tempera, June 1947.

Tow Path House, New Hope, 1948; Circulating Picture Club, 1949.

24. The Little Amish School Girl, tempera, July 1947.

Aurand Shop, 1947; Harry Salpeter Gallery, New York, 1948; P. A. Freeman, Inc., 1948; University of Florida, Tallahassee, 1948-1949; Free Library, 1950; Lancaster Country Store, Brownstown, 1950-1951; Montclair (NJ) Art Museum, 1952; The Inn, Buck Hill Falls, 1952; Folk Festival, Kutztown, 1953; Glockenspiel, Kutztown, 1955-1958; Mercersburg Academy, 1959; Universalist Church, Philadelphia, 1960; Glockenspiel, Kutztown, 1961; Art Museum, Reading, 1961; Baum Art School, 1962; Woodmere Gallery, Chestnut Hill, 1963; Town House Restaurant, Lansdale, 1963; Hazleton Art League, 1964.

25. The Coffee Pot, Tole Ware, water color and crayon, August 1947.

Pennsylvania Academy of Fine Arts, Philadelphia, 1947; Harry Salpeter Gallery, New York, 1948-1949; Distelfink Gift Shop, 1950; Lancaster Country Store, Brownstown, 1950-1951; National Arts Club, Gramercy Park, NY, 1951; Terry Nation Art Exhibit, Miami, FL, 1952; Moby Dick Book Shop, 1952; Lehigh University, 1952; Woodmere Gallery, Chestnut Hill, 1952 (Best Water Color) and 1953; Folk Festival, Kutztown, 1953; Cedar Crest College, 1955; Glockenspiel, Kutztown, 1955-1958; Lansdale Art League, 1959; Meierhans Gallery, Hagersville, 1959; Art Museum, 1960; Glockenspiel, Kutztown, 1961; Ruth Hager Gallery, Lancaster, 1961-1962;

Southern Lehigh Jr.-Sr. High School, 196 ; Woodmere Gallery, Chestnut Hill, 1963; Hazleton Art League, 1966; Art League of Ligonier Valley, Rector, 1966; Reading Museum and Art Gallery, 1966; Hook's Restaurant, 1968; Schoen's Furniture, 1969; New Britain (CT) Museum of American Art, 1955; Lehigh Art Alliance, 1975; Lehigh County Court House, 1976-78.

26. Distelfink, tempera and water color, September 1947.

Aurand Shop, 1947; Harry Salpeter Gallery, New York, 1948; Tow Path House, New Hope, 1948; Distelfink Gift Shop, 1948-1949; Circulating Picture Club, 1950-1951; Betty Seidel Shops, Cherryville, 1955; Meierhans Gallery, Hagersville, 1959.

27. The Painted Tray, tempera and crayon, November 1947.

Harry Salpeter Gallery, New York, 1948-1949; Free Library, 1950; Lancaster County Store, Brownstown, 1950-1951.

28. The Egg and I, tempera and crayon, November 1947.

Harry Salpeter Gallery, New York, 1948-1949.

29. Five Apples, tempera, December 1947.

Harry Salpeter Gallery, New York, 1948-1949; Woodmere Gallery, Chestnut Hill, 1950; Lancaster Country Store, Brownstown, 1950-1951; Art Museum, 1951; Glockenspiel, Kutztown, 1955; Little Studio, Gimbels, New York, 1955-1956; Glockenspiel, 1961; Ruth Hager Gallery, Lancaster, 1961-1962; Art Museum, 1962; Woodmere Gallery, Chestnut Hill, 1963.

30. Leaping - Quilt Horse, water color and crayon, January 1948.

Harry Salpeter Gallery, New York, 1948; Gimbel Gallery, New York and Carlebach Galleries, New York, 1948; Liberty High School, Bethlehem, 1951; Art Museum, 1951; Lehigh University, Bethlehem, 1952; Brill's Artists Supply Store, 1954; Betty Seidel Shops, Cherryville, 1955-1956; Schoen's Furniture, 1956-1958; Meierhans Gallery, Hagersville, 1959.

31. Apple Butter, tempera and crayon, February, 1948.

Harry Salpeter Gallery, New York, 1948; P. A. Freeman, Inc., 1984; Distelfink Gift Shop, 1949; Free Library, 1950; Folk Festival, Kutztown, 1950; Lancaster Country Store, Brownstown, 1950;

Liberty High School, Bethlehem, 1951; The Inn, Buck Hill Falls, 1952; Little Studio, Gimbels, New York, 1955-1956; Schoen's Furniture, 1956-1958; Meierhans Gallery, Hagersville, 1959; Mercersburg Academy, 1959.

32. Quilt Appliquè, water color and tempera, February 1948.

Harry Salpeter Gallery, New York, 1948-1949; Free Library, 1950; Tow Path House, New Hope, 1950; Circulating Picture Club, 1950-1951; Moravian College, 1969; Reading Museum, 1970.

33. Pretzels, tempera and crayon, March 1948.

Harry Salpeter Gallery, New York, 1948-1949; Free Library, 1950; Lancaster County Store, Brownstown, 1950-1951; Tow Path House, New Hope, 1951; Lehigh University, 1952; Folk Festival, Kutztown, 1953, 1955; Betty Seidel Shops, Cherryville, 1956; Kutztown University, 1957; Woman's Club, 1958; Meierhans Gallery, Hagersville, 1959; Mercersburg Academy, 1959; Universalist Church, Philadelphia, 1960; Glockenspiel, Kutztown, 1961; Ruth Hager Gallery, Lancaster, 1961-1962; Woodmere Gallery, Chestnut Hill, 1963; Hazleton Art League, 1966; Reading Museum, 1968; Hooks' Restaurant, 1968; Moravian Seminary, Green Pond, 1970; Lehigh Art Alliance, 1971; New Britain (CT) Museum of American Art, 1975; Musselman Studio, 1980.

34. Spring Landscape, tempera and water color, March 1948.

P. A. Freeman, Inc., 1948; Distelfink Gift Shop, 1948; Tow Path House, New Hope, 1949; Lansdale Art League, 1965 (Honorable Mention).

35. Cock and Hen, crayon and tempera, May 1948.

Woodmere Gallery, Chestnut Hill, 1949; Tow Path House, New Hope, 1949.

36. Thru the Bridge; Under a Bridge, tempera, May 1948.

Circulating Picture Club, 1951.

37. The Swallow House, tempera, June 1948.

Lehigh University, 1948.

38. Dutch Abstract No. 1 (Pennsylvania Dutch No. 38), tempera, July 1948; repainted February 1964.

Lehigh Art Alliance, 1964; Lansdale Art League, 1964; Muhlenberg College, 1964; Southern Lehigh High School, Coopersburg, 1965; Hazleton Art League, 1966; Lansdale Art League, 1967; Reading Museum, 1970; New Britain (CT) Museum of American Art, 1975; Lehigh County Court House, 1978; Musselman Studio, 1980.

39. Swallow Courtyard, water color and tempera, August 1948.

American Water Color Society, Philadelphia, 1949; Gallery Studio, Bethlehem, 1950; Woodmere Gallery, Chestnut Hill, 1952; Parkland High School, Orefield, 1955; Betty Seidel Shops, Cherryville, 1955; Circulating Picture Club, 1958-1959; Mercersburg Academy, 1959; Universalist Church, Philadelphia, 1960; Buck Hill Inn, Pocono Mountains, 1960; Ruth Hager Gallery, Lancaster, 1961-1962; Woodmere Gallery, 1963; Town House Restaurant, Lansdale, 1963; The Spinning Wheel, 1964; Moravian College, 1965; Hazleton Art League, 1966; Library, Emmaus, 1966-1967; Reading Museum, 1968; Hook's Restaurant, 1968; Kemmerer Museum, Bethlehem, 1973.

40. Symbols In The Night; Flying Hex Signs, water color and crayon, August 1948.

Woodmere Gallery, Chestnut Hill, 1948-1949; Tow Path House, New Hope, 1949; Don-Mart Interiors, Reading, 1950; Gallery Studio, Bethlehem, 1950; Art Museum, 1951; Lehigh University, 1952; Woodmere Gallery, 1963; Circulating Picture Club, 1978-1981.

41. Ceramics and Bottles, water color, tempera and crayon, August 1948

Regional Exhibition, Artists of Reading and Vicinity, 1963.

42. Pink Lady; Dutch Abstract No. 2, tempera and crayon, October 1948.

43. Gallery Studio; Jerry's Studio, water color, tempera, and crayon, November 1948.

44. Pink Tulips, water color, tempera and crayon, November 1948.

45. After the Storm, water color and tempera, January 1949.

Muhlenberg College, 1949; Tow Path House, New Hope, 1949; Gallery Studio, Bethlehem, 1950; Lehigh University, 1952; Moby Dick Book Shop, 1952; The Inn, Buck Hill Falls, 1952; Circulating Picture Club, Art Museum, 1953-1954; Glockenspiel, Kutztown, 1955.

46. Barn Abstraction, tempera, February 1949.

Free Library, 1950; Tow Path House, New Hope, 1950.

47. Rhythm and Squares; Birds of a Feather, tempera and crayon, March 1949.

Aurand Shop, 1950; Lehigh University, 1952; Moby Dick Book Shop, 1952; Meierhans Gallery, Hagersville, 1959.

48. Refreshers, tempera and crayon, March 1949.

Water Color Club Exhibition, Philadelphia, 1949; Art Museum, 1949; Don-Mart Interiors, Reading, 1950; Audubon Artists' Exhibition, New York, 1950; Gallery Studio, Bethlehem, 1950; Aurand Shop, 1950; Liberty High School, Bethlehem, 1951; Art Museum, 1962. Owner: Liberty High School, Bethlehem.

49. Sand Drifts, water color and crayon, June 1949.

Tow Path House, New Hope, 1950; Gallery Studio, Bethlehem, 1950; Aurand Shop, 1950; Water Color Club, Philadelphia, 1951; American Water Color Society, Exhibition, New York, 1951; Woodmere Gallery, Chestnut Hill, 1953; National Arts Club Gallery, 1954; Woodmere Gallery, 1954; Decorators Furniture Showrooms, Philadelphia, 1954-1955; Schoen's Furniture, 1956-1957; Circulating Picture Club Exhibit, 1957. Owner: Raub Junior High School, Allentown.

50. Portrait of a School Teacher (Lillian Schlogel Walter), crayon and water color, July 1949.

Gallery Studio, Bethlehem, 1950; Aurand Shop, 1950; Folk Festival, Kutztown, 1954.

51. Corn Crib; Corner of a Backyard, water color and tempera, July 1949.

Tow Path House, New Hope, 1949-1950; Gallery Studio, Bethlehem, 1950; Lancaster Country Store, Brownstone, 1950-1951; Art Museum, 1951;

Woodmere Gallery, Chestnut Hill, 1952; Lehigh University, 1952; Moby Dick Book Shop, 1952; Woodmere Gallery, 1952; Don-Mart Interiors, Reading, 1952-1953; Brill's Artists Supply Store, 1954; Betty Seidel Gift Shops, Cherryville, 1954-1955; Little Gallery Shop, Gimbels, New York, 1955-1956; Schoen's Furniture, 1956-1957; Meierhans Gallery, Hagersville, 1958; Art Museum; 1962; Woodmere Gallery, 1963; Hazleton Art League, 1966; Reading Museum, 1968; Lehigh Art Alliance, 1968.

52. Portrait of a Designer (Kenneth Bogert), water color, crayon and tempera, August 1949.

Gallery Studio, Bethlehem, 1950; Aurand Shop, 1950.

53. Portrait of My Aunt (Linda Kohler Frankenfield), water color and tempera, September 1949.

Lehigh University, 1949; Gallery Studio, Bethlehem, 1950; Aurand Shop, 1950; Folk Festival, Kutztown, 1954.

54. Dinner, Please; Good Eating, tempera, November 1949, repainted September 1966.

Gallery Studio, Bethlehem, 1950; Lehigh Art Alliance, 1966; Reading Museum, 1967; Dieruff High School, 1968; Hook's Restaurant, 1968; Woodmere Gallery, 1971; Bethlehem City Center, 1972; Circulating Picture Club, 1974, 1978-1981.

55. Portrait of a Musician, Violinist (Miriam Leeds), water color, tempera and crayon, November 1949.

Gallery Studio, Bethlehem, 1950; Aurand Shop, 1950; Liberty High School, Bethlehem.

56. A Bell Rings; A Bell Tolls, tempera and crayon, January 1950.

Water Color Club, Philadelphia, 1950; Lehigh University, 1950; Art Museum, 1951; Florida Southern College, Lakeland, FL, 1952; Woodmere Gallery, Chestnut Hill, 1954; Glockenspiel, Kutztown, 1955; Schoen's Furniture, 1957-1958.

57. Pigeon Holes, tempera and crayon, January 1950.

Gallery Studio, Bethlehem, 1950; Aurand Shop, 1950; Circulating Picture Club, 1951.

58. Pigeon Holes Abstract, tempera and water color, February 1950.

Gallery Studio, Bethlehem, 1950; Lancaster Country Store, Brownstown, 1951; Aurand Shop, 1955; Schoen's Furniture, 1956-1958.

59. A Bell Tolls - Abstract, tempera and crayon, February 1950.

Freeman's Store, 1950; Gallery Studio, Bethlehem, 1950.

60. Quilt Patterns, water color and tempera, March 1950.

Lancaster Country Store, Brownstown, 1951; Art Museum, 1951; Montclair (NJ) Museum, 1952; Folk Festival, Kutztown, 1954; Aurand Shop, 1955; Parkland High School, Orefield, 1955; Meierhans Gallery, Hagersville, 1959; Art Museum, 1962; Woodmere Gallery, Chestnut Hill, 1963; Moravian College, 1968; Hook's Restaurant, 1968.

61. Spring Blood; Bloodroots, water color and tempera, March 1950.

Muhlenberg College, 1950; Tow Path House, New Hope, 1951-1952; Don-Mart Interiors, 1952-1953.

62. Sea Fantasy; Sea Fever, water color and tempera, March 1950.

Gallery Studio, Bethlehem, 1950; Tow Path House, New Hope, 1950-1951; Lehigh University, 1952; Aurand Shop, 1955; Betty Seidel Gift Shops, Cherryville, 1955; Art Museum, 1955.

63. Shore Lines, water color, crayon and tempera, April 1950.

Gallery Studio, Bethlehem, 1950; Woodmere Gallery, Chestnut Hill, 1950 (Membership Exhibition, Second Honorable Mention); Tow Path House, New Hope, 1951; Liberty High School, 1951; Woodmere Gallery, 1951; Audubon Artists, 1952; Pace-Setter Shop, 1953; Brill's Artists Supply Store, 1954-1955; Cedar Crest College, 1955; Reading Museum, 1957; Southern Lehigh Jr.-Sr. High School, Coopersburg, 1958-1959; Meierhans Gallery, Hagersville, 1959; Lansdale Art League, 1961 (Honorable Mention, abstract); Inn, Buck Hill Falls, 1962; Woodmere Gallery, 1963.

64. Daybreak; Morning Fantasy, water color, crayon and tempera, April 1950.

Muhlenberg College, 1950; Allied Artists of America, Inc., exhibition, 1950; Kramer's Music House, 1956-1957.

65. Trillium, ink and tempera, May 1950.

Gallery Studio, Bethlehem, 1950; Aurand Shop, 1950; Circulating Picture Club, 1951.

66. Dutchman's Breeches, water color and tempera, May 1950.

Gallery Studio, Bethlehem, 1950; Liberty High School, Bethlehem, 1951; Circulating Picture Club, 1952; Aurand Shop, 1955; Glockenspiel, Kutztown, 1955; Inn, Buck Hill Falls, 1955; Faenza Coffee Shop, 1955-6; Schoen's Furniture, 1956-1958; Meierhans Gallery, 1959; Doris Fisher McCormick, Inc., Silverdale, 1960.

67. Barn - Hub of the Farm, water color, ink and tempera, July 1950; retouched with crayons and colored pencils, February 1966.

Lehigh University, 1951; Montclair (NJ) Art Museum, 1952; Art Museum, 1962; Hazleton Art League, 1966; Lansdale Art League, 1966.

68. Williamsburg Enclosures, water color, casein and ink, July 1950.

Liberty High School, Bethlehem, 1951; Art Museum, 1951; Lehigh University, Bethlehem, 1952.

69. Columbine, casein and ink, July 1950.

Liberty High School, Bethlehem, 1951; Art Museum, 1951; Lehigh University, 1952; Aurand Shop, 1955; Glockenspiel, Kutztown, 1955; Faenza Coffee Shop, 1955-1956; Schoen's Furniture, 1956-1958; Meierhans Gallery, Hagersville, 1959; Art Museum, 1962; Inn, Buck Hill Falls, 1962; Woodmere Gallery, Chestnut Hill, 1963.

70. Grandmother's Kitchen; Daily Pennsylvania Dutch Objects, Patterns, water color, casein and ink, August 1950.

Everhart Museum, Scranton, 1950; Tow Path House, New Hope, 1951; Florida Southern College, Lakeland, FL, 1952; Folk Festival, Kutztown, 1954; Betty Seidel Gift Shops, Cherryville, 1955; Faenza Coffee Shop, 1955; Schoen's Furniture, 1956-8; Meierhans Gallery, Hagersville, 1959; Mercersburg Academy, 1959; Universalist Church, Philadelphia, 1960; Art Museum, 1960; Woodmere Gallery, Chestnut Hill, 1963; Hazleton Art League, 1966; New Britain (CT) Museum of American Art, 1975; Lehigh Art Alliance, Bethlehem, 1975; Musselman Studio, 1980.

71. Pennsylvania Dutch Tombstones, India ink, September 1950.

Liberty High School, Bethlehem, 1951; Lehigh University, 1952; Folk Festival, Kutztown, 1953, 1954; Aurand Shop, 1955; Kutztown University, 1957; Meierhans Gallery, Hagersville, 1959; Hazleton Art League, 1966.

72. Sunbury Plant, casein and India ink, October 1950.

Art Museum, 1962. Owner: Pennsylvania Power and Light Co., Allentown.

73. Pulverizer, Sunbury Power Plant, casein and India ink, October 1950.

Owner: Pennsylvania Power and Light Co., Allentown.

74. Control House, Sunbury Power Plant, casein and India ink, October 1950.

Owner: Pennsylvania Power and Light Co., Allentown.

75. The Yellow Chair, casein and India ink, November 1950.

Art Museum, 1951.

76. Indian Pipes, casein and India ink, January 1951.

Art Museum, 1951; Woodmere Gallery, Chestnut Hill, 1951, 1952; Don-Mart Interiors, Reading, 1952-1953; Aurand Shop, 1955; Cedar Crest College, 1955; Schoen's Furniture, 1956-1958; Meierhans Gallery, Hagersville, 1959.

77. Bird in a Cage, crayon and India ink, March 1951.

Art Museum, 1951; Tow Path House, New Hope, 1951-1952; Don-Mart Interiors, Reading, 1952-1953; Woodmere Gallery, Chestnut Hill, 1972.

78. My Church IHS (Trinity United Church of Christ, Allentown), crayon, India ink and casein, March 1951.

Lehigh University, 1951. Owner: Good Shepherd Home.

79. The Etching Room of the Morning Call, No. 1, Portrait of the Press, crayon, India ink, and casein, April 1951.

Art Museum, 1962. Owner: Call-Chronicle Newspapers.

80. Etching Room No. 2, Motion of the Etching Process, casein and India ink, May 1951.

Owner: Call-Chronicle Newspapers.

81. Rolling Paper, Call-Chronicle Newspaper; Rolling On To The Press, casein, May 1951.

Owner: Call-Chronicle Newspapers.

82. Butter Molds, casein and crayon, May 1951.

Folk Festival, Kutztown, 1953, 1954; Parkland High School, Orefield, 1955; Faenza Coffee Shop, 1955-1956; Folk Festival, 1954; Meierhans Gallery, Hagersville, 1959; Mercersburg Academy, 1959.

83. The Artist's Challenge, India ink, casein and crayon, July 1951.

Art Museum, 1951; American Watercolor Society exhibition, New York, 1952; Harcum Junior College, Bryn Mawr, 1952; Meierhans Gallery, Hagersville, 1959; Art Museum, 1962; Woodmere Gallery, Chestnut Hill, 1963; Lansdale Art League, 1965, (Best for Genre, Junior Chamber of Commerce Medal); Association of Delaware Valley Art Centers, Philadelphia, 1965, (Philadelphia Commercial Museum Civic Center Award): Hazleton Art League, 1966; Lehigh Art Alliance, 1966 (Silver Award); Muhlenberg College, 1966; Reading Museum, 1966, 1968; Kemmerer Museum, Bethlehem, 1973; New Britain (CT) Museum of American Art, 1975; Doylestown Art League, Hagersville, 1976; Woodmere Gallery, Chestnut Hill, 1979, 1981.

84. Rising Sun Farm, Casein and India ink, October 1951.

Lehigh Valley Dairy, 1952; Water Color Club, Philadelphia, 1952.

85. Rising Sun Farm No. 2; Barn Doors, casein and crayon, November 1951.

Owner: Lehigh Valley Cooperative Dairy Farms.

86. The Electric Milker, casein, India ink, and crayon, January 1952.

87. Pigeons On a Silo, casein and crayon, February 1952.

Water Color Club, Art Alliance, Philadelphia, 1952; Kramer's Music House, 1957; Meierhans Gallery, Hagersville, 1959.

88. Gabriel and His Horn, India ink, casein, and crayon, March 1952.

Lehigh University, 1952; Moby Dick Book Shop, 1952; Water Color Club, Art Alliance, Philadelphia, 1952; Aurand Shop, 1955; Cedar Crest College, 1955; Schoen's Furniture, 1955-1958; Meierhans Gallery, Hagersville, 1959; Doris Fisher McCormick, Inc., 1960; Glockenspiel, Kutztown, 1960; Ruth Hager Gallery, Lancaster, 1961-1962; Rose and Briar Coffee House, Bethlehem, 1964; Hazleton Art League, 1966; Schoen's Furniture, 1969.

89. The Lamp, Lamp Lines, casein, India ink and crayon, March 1952.

90. Rising Sun, casein and crayon, April 1952.

Folk Festival, Kutztown, 1952; Pennsylvania Dutch Seminar, Wernersville, 1952; Folk Festival, Selinsgrove, 1952; Woodmere Gallery, Chestnut Hill, 1952; Folk Festival, Kutztown, 1954; Meierhans Gallery, Hagersville, 1959; Mercersburg Academy, 1959; Doris Fishel McCormick, Inc., 1960; Southern Lehigh School, Coopersburg, 1961-1962; Woodmere Gallery, 1963.

91. Three Fishes, casein and India ink, May 1952.

Lehigh University, 1952; Pace-Setter Shop, 1952; Aurand Shop, 1955; Betty Seidel Gift Shops, Cherryville, 1955. Owner: Allentown State Hospital.

92. Proud Papa; Three Birds, casein and India ink, June 1952.

Pace-Setter Shop, 1952; Decorators Furniture Showroom, Philadelphia, 1955; Schoen's Furniture, 1958; Meierhans Gallery, Hagersville, 1959; Mercersburg Academy, 1959; Southern Lehigh High School, Center Valley, 1959-60.

93. Dry Milk, casein and crayon, July 1952.

94. Modern Decor, casein and crayon, November 1952.

Pace-Setter Shop, 1953; Southern Lehigh School, 1960.

95. Wings, India ink, crayon and water color, January 1953.

Water Color Club, Art Alliance, Philadelphia, 1953; Parkland High School, Orefield, 1955; Schoen's Furniture, 1958; Meierhans Gallery, Hagersville, 1959; Doris Fisher McCormick, Inc., 1960; Ruth Hager Gallery, Lancaster, 1961-1962; Lansdale Art League, 1965; Commercial Museum, Philadelphia, 1965; Hazleton Art League, 1966; Lehigh County Cultural Center and Museum, 1970; Moravian College, 1970; Circulating Picture Club, 1970.

96. Red Chimney, India ink, water color and crayon, February 1953.

Water Color Club, Art Alliance, Philadelphia, 1953; Woodmere Gallery, Chestnut Hill, 1963.

97. Creation, casein and pencil, February 1953; repainted August 1963.

Liberty High School, 1953; Woodmere Gallery, Chestnut Hill, 1963; Baum School Gallery, 1964; Lansdale Art League, 1964; Art Museum, 1964; Moravian College, 1966; Hazleton Art League, 1966; Reading Museum, 1967.

98. Neighborhood Nocturne; Roof Tops, water color and pencil, April 1953.

Woodmere Gallery, Chestnut Hill, 1954; National Society of Painters in Casein, New York, 1955; Kutztown University, 1957; Woodmere Gallery, 1963; Lehigh Art Alliance, 1978; Circulating Picture Club, 1978.

99. Tree Root, casein and crayon, May 1953.

Decorators Furniture Showrooms, Philadelphia, 1955; Southern Lehigh School, Center Valley, 1956; Schoen's Furniture, 1956.

100. Anthracite; Portrait of Anthracite, water color, casein and crayon, July 1953.

Lehigh Coal and Navigation Co.

101. Productive Forces, casein, India ink and crayon, September 1953.

Audubon Arts Exhibition, 1953; Water Color Club, Philadelphia, Art Alliance, 1954; Kutztown University, 1957; Hazleton Art League, 1966; Dieruff High School, 1966; Museum of Philadelphia Civic Center, 1966; Southern Lehigh High School, Coopersburg, 1967; Pennational Arts, Ligonier, 1967; Woodmere Gallery, Chestnut Hill, 1967; Reading Museum, 1968; Bethlehem City Center, 1968-1969; Schoen's, 1969; Bethlehem City Center, 1972.

102. Perce Rock, water color, India ink and crayon, November 1953.

Aurand Shop, 1955; Kramer's Music House, 1956-1957; Kutztown University, 1957; Meierhans Gallery, Hagersville, 1959; Art Museum, 1962; Woodmere Gallery, Chestnut Hill, 1963; Moravian College, 1963; Circulating Picture Club, 1977-1981.

103. Pennsylvania Dutch 103, India ink, crayon and casein, December 1953.

Liberty High School, Bethlehem, 1954; Folk Festival, Kutztown, 1954; Cedar Crest College, 1955; Little Studio, Gimbels, New York, 1955-1956; Lansdale Art League, 1956; The Conovers, 1965; Southern Lehigh High School, 1957; Folk Festival, Kutztown, 1957; Meierhans Gallery, Hagersville, 1959; Mercersburg Academy, 1959; Universalist Church, Philadelphia, 1960; Glockenspiel, Kutztown, 1961; Ruth Hager Gallery, Lancaster, 1961-1962; Woodmere Gallery, Chestnut Hill, 1963.

104. Lower Town, water color and crayon, January 1954.

Lehigh University, 1954; Water Color Club, Art Alliance, Philadelphia, 1954; Audubon Artists, National Academy Galleries, New York, 1955; Lansdale Art League, 1956; Schoen's Furniture, 1956-1957; Southern Lehigh School, Coopersburg, 1958; Reading Museum, 1958; Woodmere Gallery, Chestnut Hill, 1959; Lehigh Art Alliance, 1959; Mercersburg Academy, 1959; Universalist Church, Philadelphia, 1960; Inn, Buck Hill Falls, 1960; Engineer's Club, Philadelphia, 1961; Art Museum, 1961 (one man show award); Ruth Hager Gallery, Lancaster, 1961-1962; Wyoming Valley Art League, Wilkes-Barre, 1962; Baum Art School, 1962; Dave Zeswitz Music Center, Reading, 1962; Everhart Museum, Scranton, 1962; Woodmere Gallery, 1963; Buxmont Regional Art Committee Exhibition, Souderton, 1964 (First Prize, professional class); Hazleton Art League, 1965 (Purchase prize).

105. Pennsylvania Dutch Tree, casein and crayon, April 1954.

Folk Festival, Kutztown, 1954; Aurand Shop, 1955; Little Studio, Gimbels, New York, 1956; Glockenspiel, Kutztown, 1961; Reading Museum, 1968.

106. Portrait of Allentown, casein and crayon, April 1954.

Muhlenberg College, 1954; Circulating Picture Club, 1954-1955; Kramer's Music House, 1956.

107. Pennsylvania Dutch Block Heads, casein and colored pencil, June 1954.

Water Color Club, 1954; Liberty High School, Bethlehem, 1955; Little Studio, Gimbels, New York, 1956; Schoen's Furniture, 1956-1957; Meierhans Gallery, Hagersville, 1959; Universalist Church, Philadelphia, 1960; Glockenspiel, Kutztown, 1961; Woodmere

Gallery, Chestnut Hill, 1970; Dieruff High School, 1972; New Britain (CT) Museum of American Art, 1975; Lehigh Art Alliance, 1976.

108. Pennsylvania Dutch Farm, casein, crayon and colored pencil, September 1954.

Lehigh Art Alliance, 1954; Liberty High School, Bethlehem, 1955; Knickerbacher Artists Exhibition, Riverside Museum, New York, 1955 (M. Grumbacher prize for casein merchandise); Muhlenberg College, 1955; Folk Festival, Kutztown, 1955; Water Color Club, Pennsylvania Academy of Fine Arts, Philadelphia, 1955. Owner: Butler Institute of American Art, Youngstown, OH.

109. Pennsylvania Brick End Barns, water color and casein, October 1954.

Folk Festival, Kutztown, 1955.

110. In a Pennsylvania Dutch Kitchen, casein and crayon, January 1955.

Water Color Club, Art Alliance, Philadelphia, 1955; Little Studio, Gimbels, New York, 1956; Schoen's Furniture, 1956-1958; Glockenspiel, Kutztown, 1960; Doris Fisher McCormick, Silverdale, 1960.

111. Plain and Fancy, casein and crayon, February 1955.

112. Allentown, Pennsylvania, casein and crayon, May 1955; repainted April 1962.

Muhlenberg College, 1955; Allentown Bi-Centennial Celebration, 1962 (Critics Choice); Free Library, 1962; Kutztown University, 1962; Albright College, 1962; Hazleton Art League, 1962; Art Museum, 1970; Annie S. Kemmerer Museum, 1985.

113. Wings; Canary and Blue Wings, casein and crayon, May 1955; retouched with crayon and colored pencil, 1966.

Woodmere Gallery, Chestnut Hill, 1955; Regional Council of Community Art Centers, 1955 (Honorable Mention for professional artists); Woodmere Gallery, 1956; Schoen's Furniture, 1956; Art Museum, 1957; Meierhans Gallery, Hagersville, 1959; Universalist Church, Philadelphia, 1960; Buck Hill Inn, 1969; Hazleton Art League, 1966; Art Museum, 1966; Reading Museum, 1968; Schoen's, 1969; Lehigh County Cultural Center, 1970; Dieruff High School, 1970; Woodmere Gallery, 1973; Moravian College, 1974; (Lehigh Art Alliance Critics Choice) Lehigh Art Alliance, 1975; Woodmere Gallery, 1981; Muhlenberg College, 1985.

114. Stover's Mill (Bucks County), No. 1, casein and crayon, June 1955.

Southern Lehigh High School, Center Valley, 1955-1956; Schoen's Furniture, 1956-1958; Art Museum, 1958-1962; Woodmere Gallery, Chestnut Hill, 1963; Circulating Picture Club, 1978.

115. Stover's Mill (Bucks County) No. 2, casein and crayon, July 1955.

Schoen's Furniture, 1956-1958; Meierhans Gallery, Hagersville, 1959; Doris Fisher McCormick Inc., Silverdale, 1960; Southern Lehigh High School, Center Valley, 1960; The Spinning Wheel, 1960.

116. Pennsylvania Wrought Iron, casein and crayon, July 1955.

117. Pennsylvania Dutch Brick End Barns, No. 2, casein and crayon, September 1955.

Lansdale Art League, 1956; Kutztown University, 1957; Folk Festival, Kutztown, 1957; Mercersburg Academy, 1959; Universalist Church, Philadelphia, 1960; Glockenspiel, Kutztown, 1961; Ruth Hager Gallery, Lancaster, 1961-1962; Lansdale Art League, 1964; Allen High School, 1964; Moravian Seminary, Green Pond, 1970.

118. Primeval Days, White Cloud (Indian Abstract), India ink, crayon and casein, January 1956.

Schoen's Furniture, 1956; Audubon Artists Show, National Academy Galleries, New York, 1957; Meierhans Gallery, Hagersville, 1959; Lansdale Art League, 1966; Southern Lehigh School, Coopersburg, 1966; Hazleton Art League, 1967; Woodmere Gallery, Chestnut Hill, 1974; Circulating Picture Club, 1975-1978.

119. Indian Trails, India ink, casein and crayon, January 1956.

Liberty High School, Bethlehem, 1956; Schoen's Furniture, 1957; Meierhans Gallery, Hagersville, 1959; Woodmere Gallery, Chestnut Hill, 1963; Lansdale Art League, 1963; Southern Lehigh School, Coopersburg, 1963-1964; Art Museum, 1964; Hazleton Art League, 1966; Reading Museum, 1968; Muhlenberg College, 1968; Bethlehem City Center, 1968-1969; Woodmere Gallery, 1976; Circulating Picture Club, 1978.

120. Sanctus; A Broken Body, casein, India ink and crayon, February 1956.

Liberty High School, Bethlehem, 1956; Lansdale Art League, 1956; Kutztown University, 1957; Meierhans Gallery, Hagersville, 1959. Owner: Good Shepherd Home.

121. Potted Plant, casein, crayon, and India ink, March 1956.
Schoen's Furniture, 1956-1958; Circulating Picture Club, 1958-1959.

122. Spring In Pennsylvania, casein and crayon, April 1956.
Water Color Club, Art Alliance, Philadelphia, 1956; Schoen's Furniture, 1956; Folk Festival, Kutztown, 1957; Meierhans Gallery, Hagersville, 1959; Art Museum, 1962; Buck Hill Inn, 1962; Woodmere Gallery, Chestnut Hill, 1963.

123. Lighthouse; Light in the Night, casein and crayon, May 1956.
Woodmere Gallery, Chestnut Hill, 1956; American Watercolor Society, 1957; Woodmere Gallery, 1957; Aurand's Shop, 1958; Circulating Picture Club, 1958-59.

124. Souvenirs, casein and crayon, June 1956.
Schoen's Furniture, 1956; Kutztown University, 1957; Meierhans Gallery, Hagersville, 1959; Doris Fisher McCormick, Inc., Silverdale, 1960; Southern Lehigh High School, Center Valley, 1961; Allen High School, 1964; Circulating Picture Club, 1978.

125. Decoys, casein and crayon, July 1956.
Schoen's Furniture, 1956; Lehigh University, 1956; Liberty High School, Bethlehem, 1956-1957; Kutztown University, 1957; Meierhans Gallery, Hagersville, 1959; The Inn, Buck Hill Falls, 1959; Doris Fisher McCormick, Inc., Silverdale, 1960; Circulating Picture Club, 1961; Art Museum, 1962; Woodmere Gallery, Chestnut Hill, 1963; Circulating Picture Club, 1978.

126. Pennsylvania Dutch Summer House, casein and crayon, July 1956.

127. Chickens, casein and crayon, August 1956.
Art Museum, 1957; Lansdale Art League, 1961 (Honorable Mention in professional group); Art Museum, 1962; Zeswitz Music Center, Reading, 1962; Buxmont Regional Art Committee Exhibition, Souderton, 1962; Baum Art School, 1962; Woodmere Gallery, Chestnut Hill, 1963; Owner: Schnecksville School, Parkland District, Orefield.

128. Studio Forms, No. 1, casein and crayon, October 1956.
Kutztown University, 1957; Lansdale Art League, 1957 (Honorable mention); Woodmere Gallery,

Chestnut Hill, 1957, 1958; Reading Museum, 1958; Meierhans Gallery, Hagersville, 1959; Universalist Church, Philadelphia, 1960; Art Museum, 1961; Baum Art School, 1962; Woodmere Gallery, 1963; Moravian College, 1964 (Second Prize, Watercolor); Southern Lehigh School, Coopersburg, 1964; Buxmont Regional Art Committee, Souderton, 1964; Hazleton Art League, 1966; Reading Museum, 1968; Circulating Picture Club, 1978.

129. Sticks and Stones, casein and crayon, November 1956.
Academy of Fine Arts, 1957; Kutztown University, 1957; Lansdale Art League, 1957; Art Museum; Water Color Club, Philadelphia, 1958; Meierhans Gallery, Hagersville, 1959; Mercersburg Academy, 1959; Art Museum, 1960; Buck Hill Inn, 1961; Ruth Hager Gallery, Lancaster, 1961-1962; Woodmere Gallery, Chestnut Hill, 1962 (Honorable Mention); Hazleton Art League, 1962 (One of three best in show); Woodmere Gallery, 1962; Buxmont Regional Art Committee, Souderton, 1962; Woodmere Gallery, 1963; Lehigh Art Alliance, 1963 (Honorable Mention); Lehigh Art Alliance, 1963; Pennational Artists Annual, Ligonier, 1963; Buxmont Regional, 1963 (Second prize, professional); Motorola Nonprofessional Regional Exhibit, 1968; Reading Museum, 1964; Dieruff High School, 1965; Hazleton Art League, 1966; Reading Museum, 1968; Bethlehem City Center, 1972; Circulating Picture Club, 1975.

130. Beach Forms, casein and crayon, January 1957.
Lansdale Art League, 1957; Aurand Shop, 1958; Meierhans Gallery, Hagersville, 1959.

131. The Exhibition, casein and crayon, January 1957.
Aurand's Shop, 1958; Southern Lehigh School, Coopersburg, 1959; Art Museum, 1962; Lansdale Art League, 1962; Reading Museum, 1962; Woodmere Gallery, Chestnut Hill, 1963; Hazleton Art League, 1966; Moravian Seminary, Green Pond, 1970; Moravian College, 1972; Dieruff School, 1976; Circulating Picture Club, 1978.

132. Birds, casein and crayon, March 1957.
Lansdale Art League, 1957; Liberty High School, Bethlehem, 1957; Reading Museum, 1957.

133. Schnipples, Pennsylvania Dutch Paper Cuttings, cut out paper, crayon and India ink, April 1957.
Meierhans Gallery, Hagersville, 1959.

134. Cider, India ink and crayon, May 1957.
Lehigh University, 1957; Aurand's Shop, 1958; Meierhans Gallery, Hagersville, 1959; The Glockenspiel, Kutztown, 1961; Art Museum, 1962; Moravian College, 1972; Circulating Picture Club, 1978.

135. Odds and Ends, casein and crayon, May 1957.
Water Color Club, Academy of Fine Arts, Philadelphia, 1957; Public Library, 1958; Lansdale Art League, 1958; Aurand's Shop, 1958; Meierhans Gallery, Hagersville, 1959; Universalist Church, Philadelphia, 1960; Lehigh Art Alliance, 1961; Ruth Hager Art Gallery, Lancaster, 1961-1962; Baum High School, 1962; Woodmere Gallery, Chestnut Hill, 1963; Town House Restaurant, Lansdale, 1963; Rose and Briar Coffee House, Bethlehem, 1964; Spinning Wheel, 1964; Hazleton Art League, 1966; Reading Museum, 1968; Moravian Seminary, Green Pond, 1970; Dieruff School, 1976; Circulating Picture Club, 1978.

136. The United Way, casein and crayon, June 1957.
State Museum, 1957. Owner: United Community Chest and Community Council.

137. Heart of the Community, The United Way, casein and crayon, June 1957.
State Museum, 1957. Owner: United Community Chest and Community Council.

138. Seaport USA, Rockport, casein and crayon, July 1957.
Water Color Club, Academy of Fine Arts, Philadelphia, 1957; Lehigh University and Liberty High School, Bethlehem, 1958; Aurand's Shop, 1958; Woodmere Gallery, Chestnut Hill, 1959; Meierhans Gallery, Hagersville, 1959; Universalist Church, Philadelphia, 1960; Ruth Hager Art Gallery, Lancaster, 1962; Woodmere Gallery, 1963; Spinning Wheel, 1964; Pennational Artists Annual, Ligonier, 1965; Lansdale Art League, 1965; Reading Museum, 1966; Dieruff High School, 1968; Moravian Seminary, Green Pond, 1970; Circulating Picture Club, 1978.

139. Boy Scouts, casein and crayon, August 1957.

State Museum, Harrisburg, 1957.

140. Moravian College, casein and crayon, August 1957.

Moravian College, 1957 (Second Prize). Owner: Moravian College.

141. The White Table, casein, India ink and crayon, September 1957.

Water Color Club, Art Alliance, Philadelphia, 1958; Woodmere Gallery, Chestnut Hill, 1963; Hazleton Art League, 1970; Lehigh Art Alliance, 1970; Art Museum, 1971; Dieruff High School, 1972; Kemmerer Museum, Bethlehem, 1972; Reading Museum, 1972; Circulating Picture Club, 1975.

142. From the Orient, casein and crayon, November 1957.

Lansdale Art Exhibition, 1957 (Best Abstract); Lansdale Art League, 1958; Water Color Club, Art Alliance, Philadelphia, 1958; Lehigh University and Liberty High School, Bethlehem, 1958; Meierhans Gallery, Hagersville, 1959; Art Museum, 1960; Hazleton Art League, 1961; Ruth Hager Art Gallery, Lancaster, 1962; Reading Museum, 1962; Woodmere Gallery, Chestnut Hill, 1963; Town House Restaurant, Lansdale, 1963; Hazleton Art League, 1966; Dieruff High School, 1967; Reading Museum, 1968; Moravian College, 1968 (First Prize). Owner: Moravian College.

143. In the Garden, An Artist's Dream, Tree Root and Birds, casein and crayon, January 1958.

Aurand's Shop, 1958; Meierhans Gallery, Hagersville, 1959; Circulating Picture Club, 1978.

144. First National Bank, casein and crayon, February 1958.

Owner: First National Bank.

145. Barn Signs, casein and crayon, March 1958.

Aurand's Shop, 1958; Glockenspiel, Kutztown, 1960.

146. Trio, casein and crayon, April 1958.

Aurand's Shop, 1958; Glockenspiel, Kutztown, 1960; Doris Fisher McCormick, Inc., Silverdale, 1960; Dieruff High School, 1976; Circulating Picture Club, 1978.

147. Antiques, casein and crayon, May 1958.

Aurand's Shop, 1958; Lansdale Art League, 1959 (Honorable Mention, Still Life; Kiwanis Award); Meierhans Gallery, Hagersville, 1959; Mercersburg Academy, 1959; Woodmere Gallery, Chestnut Hill, 1960; Glockenspiel, Kutztown, 1961; Ruth Hager Gallery, Lancaster, 1962; Circulating Picture Club, 1962.

148. Circus Color, casein and crayon, June 1958.

Aurand's Shop, 1958.

149. Illusion, casein and crayon, July 1958.

Aurand's Shop, 1958; Lansdale Art League, 1958; Woodmere Gallery, Chestnut Hill, 1959; Meierhans Gallery, Hagersville, 1959.

150. Masks, casein and crayon, 1958.

Woodmere Gallery, Chestnut Hill, 1958; Meierhans Gallery, Hagersville, 1959; Doris Fisher McCormick, Inc., Silverdale, 1960.

151. Sails In The Sun, casein and crayon, September 1958.

Moravian Seminary, Green Pond, 1970.

152. Tables-Interior, India ink and crayon, October 1958.

153. Antique Clocks, India ink and crayon, February 1959.

Lansdale Art League, 1959; Lehigh University, 1959; Glockenspiel, Kutztown, 1961; Ruth Hager Gallery, Lancaster, 1962; Woodmere Gallery, Chestnut Hill, 1963;; Circulating Picture Club, 1978.

154. Studio Corner, India ink and crayon, April 1959.

Reading Museum, 1959; Allen High School, 1964; Hazleton Art League, 1966; Lansdale Art League, 1968; Moravian Seminary, Green Pond, 1978.

155. Barns, casein and crayon, May 1959.

Reading Museum, 1959; Lansdale Art League, 1960 (Honorable Mention); Glockenspiel, Kutztown, 1961; Ruth Hager Gallery, Lancaster, 1961; Hazleton Art League, 1966; Moravian Seminary, Green Pond, 1970; Art Museum, 1971; Circulating Picture Club, 1971.

156. Whitetop Table, casein and crayon, June 1959.

Woodmere Gallery, Chestnut Hill, 1959.

157. Wild Flowers, casein, India ink, and crayon, July 1959.

Doris Fisher McCormick, Inc., Silverdale, 1960; Ruth Hager Gallery, Lancaster, 1961; Southern Lehigh School, Coopersburg, 1964; Circulating Picture Club, 1970.

158. Pennsylvania Landscape, India ink and crayon, August 1959.

Moravian College, 1959; Lansdale Art League, 1960; Southern Lehigh School, Coopersburg, 1962-1963; Reading Museum, 1964; Hazleton Art League, 1966; Art Museum, 1969; Bloomsburg University, 1970.

159. Antique Table, India ink and crayon, September 1959.

Lansdale Art League, 1960; Baum School, 1960; Glockenspiel, Kutztown, 1961; Art Museum, 1962; Circulating Picture Club, 1962.

160. Looking Upward, Freedom or Darkness, India ink and crayon, January 1960.

Lehigh Art Alliance, 1960; Leh's Store, 1960; State Museum, Harrisburg, 1960; Owner: Liberty Bell Shrine.

161. Trio No. 1, India ink and crayon, February 1960.

Circulating Picture Club, 1962.

162. Three Freedoms: Worship, Communication, Assembly, India ink and crayon, February 1960.

Lehigh Art Alliance, 1960; Leh's Store, 1960; State Museum, Harrisburg, 1960.

163. Trio No. 2, India ink and crayon, March 1960.

Lehigh Art Alliance, 1960 (Silver Award); Regional Council, Community Art Centers, 1960 (Second Prize, professional); Hazleton Art League, 1961; Glockenspiel, Kutztown, 1960; Buck Hill Inn, 1961; Ruth Hager Gallery, Lancaster, 1961.

164. Tulip Tree, India ink and crayon, April 1960.

Glockenspiel, Kutztown, 1961.

165. Acres of Tulips, candle wax, crayon and India ink, June 1960.

Woodmere Gallery, Chestnut Hill, 1960; Glockenspiel, Kutztown, 1961; Reading Museum, 1961; Baum School, 1962; Woodmere Gallery, 1963; Rose and Briar Coffee House, Bethlehem, 1964; Spinning Wheel, 1964; Moravian College, 1965; Hazleton Art League, 1966; Schoen's Furniture, 1969; Art Museum, 1971.

166. Fish Frolic, candle wax, crayon and India ink, June 1960.

Lehigh University, 1960; Lansdale Art League, 1961; Ruth Hager Gallery, Lancaster, 1962; Woodmere Gallery, Chestnut Hill, 1963.

167. Motif No. 1 (1), candle wax and ink, July 1960.

168. Motif No. 2 (2), ink, July 1960.

169. Lamps, casein and crayon, July 1960.

Allen High School, 1964; Moravian Seminary, Green Pond, 1970; Circulating Picture Club, 1978.

170. Snowbound, casein and crayon, August 1960.

Moravian College, 1960; Glockenspiel, Kutztown, 1961; Buck Hill Inn, 1961.

171. Flower Pot, casein, wax, and crayon, September 1960.

Baum School, 1960.

172. Radio Alarm, casein and crayon, January 1961.

173. Fish Promenade, India ink and wax, February 1961.

174. The Orange Bowl - The Window, casein and crayon, March 1961.

Art Museum, 1961; Woodmere Gallery, Chestnut Hill, 1961; Baum School, 1962; Woodmere Gallery, 1962; Woodmere Gallery, 1963; Lansdale Art League, 1963 (Kiwanis Medal for Still Life); Reading Museum, 1963; Hazleton Art League, 1964; Muhlenberg College, 1965; Zollinger-Harned Store, 1965.

175. Bird Cage, casein and crayon, September 1961.

Water Color Club, Academy of Fine Arts, Philadelphia, 1961; Lehigh Art Alliance, 1962.

176. Geometric No. 1 - Windows, casein and crayon, November 1961.

Art Museum, 1962; Woodmere Gallery, Chestnut Hill, 1963; Lansdale Art League, 1964; Allen High School, 1964-1965; Muhlenberg College, 1968; Moravian Seminary, Green Pond, 1970; Circulating Picture Club, 1974.

177. Geometric No. 2 - Cross Word Puzzles and Green Stamps, casein and crayon, December 1961.

Art Museum, 1962; Lansdale Art League, 1962 (Honorable Mention); Woodmere Gallery, Chestnut Hill, 1962; Lansdale Art League, 1963; Spinning Wheel, 1964; Muhlenberg College, 1965; Hazleton Art League, 1966; Southern Lehigh School, 1966-1967; Reading Museum, 1968; Moravian Seminary, Green Pond, 1970; Moravian College, 1973; Circulating Picture Club, 1974.

178. Geometric No. 3 - Tail Light, casein and crayon, January 1962.

179. Salt, Pepper and Sugar, casein and crayon, January 1962.

Art Museum, 1962; Woodmere Gallery, Chestnut Hill, 1963.

180. Stop, Caution and Go, casein and crayon, February 1962.

Reading Museum, 1964.

181. Allentown - Pennsylvania German Heritage, casein and crayon, March 1962

Allentown Bicentennial, 1962

182. Geometric No. 4, casein and crayon, July 1962.

Baum School, 1962; Woodmere Gallery, Chestnut Hill, 1963.

183. Studio Forms No. 2, casein and crayon, July 1962.

Moravian College, 1962; Woodmere Gallery, Chestnut Hill, 1963; Town House Restaurant, Lansdale, 1963; Art Museum, 1963; Reading Museum, 1963; Pennational Artists Exhibitions, Ligonier, 1964; Allen High School, 1964; Hazleton Art League, 1966; Lansdale Art League, 1968; Moravian Seminary, Green Pond, 1970.

184. Good Morning, casein and crayon, June 1963; retouched 1966.

Buxmont Regional, Souderton, 1963; Baum School, 1964; Art Museum, 1964; Muhlenberg College, 1965; Hazleton Art League, 1966; Dieruff High School, 1966; Civic Center Museum, Philadelphia, 1966; Woodmere Gallery, Chestnut Hill, 1966; Moravian College, 1967; Woodmere Gallery, 1967; Bethlehem City Center, 1972; Lehigh Art Alliance, 1975 (Honorable mention); Woodmere Gallery, 1981; Mountain House, Lake Mohonk, New York, 1986.

185. Pennsylvania Dutch No. 185, casein and crayon, August 1964.

Art Alliance, 1965; Muhlenberg College, 1965; Reading Museum, 1965; Hazleton Art League, 1966; Lansdale Art League, 1967; Regional Council of Community Art Centers, Philadelphia, 1967; Reading Museum, 1968; Moravian College, 1968; Bethlehem City Center, 1968-1969; Woodmere Gallery, Chestnut Hill, 1970.

186. Pennsylvania Dutch No. 186, casein and crayon, October 1964.

Southern Lehigh School, Coopersburg, 1966; Musselman Studio, 1980.

187. Pennsylvania Dutch No. 187, casein and crayon, January 1965.

Reading Museum, 1965; Hazleton Art League, 1966; Art Museum, 1969; Woodmere Gallery, Chestnut Hill, 1970.

188. Pennsylvania Dutch No. 188, buttons, casein and crayon, March 1965.

Art Museum, 1965; Buxmont Regional, Souderton, 1965; Hazleton Art League, 1966; Southern Lehigh School, 1967-1968; Reading Museum, 1968; Woodmere Gallery, Chestnut Hill, 1968; Moravian Seminary, Green Pond, 1970; Dieruff School, 1970; Lehigh Art Alliance, 1976.

189. Pennsylvania Dutch No. 189, casein, crayon, and buttons, May 1965.

Moravian College, 1965 (Second prize, watercolor); Hazleton Art League, 1966; Woodmere Gallery, Chestnut Hill, 1966; Art Museum, 1966; Dieruff High School, 1967; Lansdale Art League (Second prize); Philadelphia Civic Center, 1967; Reading Museum, 1968; Bethlehem City Center, 1969; Moravian Seminary, Green Pond, 1970; New Britain (CT) Museum of American Life, 1975; Lehigh County Museum, 1975-1976; Doylestown Art League, 1976 (second best); Woodmere Gallery, 1979; Phillips Mill, New Hope, PA, 1981; Mountain House, Lake Mohonk, NY, 1986.